Trees Don't
Grow to the Sky

Trees Don't Grow to the Sky

The Fundamentals of Product Lifecycle Management

MATTHEW FITZGERALD

ABOUT THE TITLE

"Trees don't grow to the sky" is a business adage taken from a German proverb, warning against straight-line thinking. The product, the customer, the market will not continue to grow simply because they have always grown in the past.

DEDICATION

CONTENTS

Figure 1.1 Product Lifecycle Guidance

	Launch Gain Traction	Growth Maximize Revenue	Maturity Prolong Profitability	Decline Manage Descent
Environment	• Exclusivity • Premium based on Value Prop • Low market awareness	• Competition → price decline • Sales tipping point • Market pull	• Product standardization • Many competitors • Prices fall to minimal margin	• Some competitors exit • Price-sensitive market • Declining revenue, profit
Success Keys	• Thorough planning • Violent execution • Price: premium v. adoption	• Maximize sales • Protect exclusivity • Capacity > Demand	• Maximize GM$ • Compete on value (v. price) • Improve cost position	• Salvage relationships • Minimize financial exposure • Minimum cost position

Actions	• Facilitate the ecosystem
	• Engage customers
	• Ensure availability, quality
	• Overcome competitive response
	• Validate the Value Prop
	• Org readiness
	  ○ Sales
	  ○ Customer Service
	  ○ Field Support
	  ○ Product Collateral
	• IP Strategy
	• Manage channels
	• Respond to feedback
		• Develop the ecosystem
		• Evangelize the Value Prop
		• Sell more to existing customers
		• Identify new customers
		• Enforce IP & barriers to entry
		• Respond to competitive threats
		• Resolve quality issues
		• Enhance Value Prop
		• Expand channel strategy
		• Fine tune pricing
		• Start improving costs
			• Improve all lines of P&L
			• Seek possible differentiation
			• Complexity: cost v. value
			• Capacity based on ROI
			• Minimal innovation
			• Revisit price v. share
			• Consolidate channels
			• Prune unprofitable SKUs
			• Validate P&L accuracy
				• Reduce all costs
				• Raise price
				• Standardize products
				• Transition customers
				• Manage inventory
				• Manage exit

Chapter 1
DECISIONS, DECISIONS

"If you don't know where you are going, you might wind up someplace else." Yogi Berra

It is the job of the Product Manager to drive the product lifecycle to maximize profitability over the life of the product.

A few years ago, I was invited to participate in a cross-company think tank on the topic of evaluation metrics for Product Management. How does an organization measure the effectiveness of the Product Management function? What does success look like?

This inevitably led to a discussion of the usual product line metrics, such as First Year Product Sales, hit rate on product development milestones, NPV delivered, as well as the usual operations metrics and, of course, financial outcomes such as Revenue and Gross Margin. I found all of these to be useful, but less than satisfying. First, they are all trailing edge, after-the-fact indicators. They could tell you *how* you did, but not *why*. They could tell you the final score, but not what happened during the game. Further, they are all heavily influenced by extrinsic factors. Was Revenue better than the plan simply because the market was up? Was this a case of, "all boats rise with the tide"? Did our top customer just happen to buy more, not because of anything we did? Were we simply in the right place at the right time? Should we have done *even better*? Alternatively, did we expend herculean efforts to

1

navigate unforeseen headwinds, making all the right course adjustments, only to miss a target that, in hindsight, was never really achievable? Did we do *better* than these results indicate?

Most of the conventional metrics will tell us whether we won or lost, which of course is hugely important, but not whether we did the right things. And if the scorecard only tells us what happened, not why it is happening, might it incentivize the wrong behaviors? Might a target of First Year Product Sales Revenue, for example, incent a Product Manager to lower price to drive higher volume, surrendering a price premium that may never be recovered?

Not to downplay the importance of the balanced scorecard, but back to the original question: What does effective Product Management look like? As I considered these things, my thoughts changed from, "What should we measure?" to, "What strengths should we have?" We want great results – we want the *best* results – but before great results we need the right behaviors. So, to ask the question a different way, what is the *one thing* at which Product Managers should excel? If we could pick one skill, trait, ability, or proficiency for our team, what would it be? Financial acumen? Data analysis? Customer relations? Leading and influencing others? All are important, but what is the *one thing?*

Here we should say a few words about the Product Manager role. Imagine if we expressed the business purpose of each functional group as a single scorecard metric. Sales would be Revenue, Manufacturing would be total production output, Technology would be some measure of development milestones hit, or new products released.

Product Management would be *profitability*.

The Product Manager's role is to drive the P&L to maximize short- and long-term profitability. And if profitability is the destination, then we need the path that leads there. We have to make choices about where to turn, how fast to go, and what to do when obstacles appear or the path isn't clear.

And so, I finally settled on…*decisions*. If our team could excel at one thing, it would be making good decisions, at the right time, often without all the information. Product Management is about making the best decisions, sometimes countless small ones, sometimes a handful of huge ones, to get the best possible result, as measured by short- and long-term profitability. It's about balancing risk and reward, about understanding possible outcomes, about establishing and adapting the long-term strategy and the short-range tactics. It's about knowing where we are, where we are headed, and what environment we are in. And all of these relate back to understanding the product lifecycle.

We have to know where we are, because the right decisions depend on our starting point. Adding capacity for a product in the Growth phase may make sense, but the same decision may no longer be prudent if the product is in the Mature phase.

We have to know where we want to go. What is the strategy? What are we trying to accomplish? Are we pricing to get a premium in the market, or for rapid product adoption? What kind of barriers to entry should we create? How can we differentiate? Can we innovate our Mature product back into the Growth phase? Or, is it time to minimize costs and harvest the remaining profit as we hunker down and fight off Decline and Obsolescence?

We have to know the environment. Our products don't live in a vacuum. What is happening with competitors, with customers, with regulations, standards, and funding? Is our new product new to the market, or just new to us? Is the ecosystem established and pulling the product into the market, or is it undeveloped, and we are pushing a rope? If we think of the environment as weather conditions, what do we need to prepare for? Is the weather forecast for snow and ice, or sunny and mild? Also let's keep in mind the weather forecast is never 100% accurate.

Finally, we must be well-versed in the fundamentals. If we don't understand the fundamentals of product lifecycle management, then how can we reasonably anticipate the possible outcomes of a decision?

At the end of it all, that is the point of this book. We need to understand the fundamentals of the product lifecycle so we can have the best chance to make the right decisions based on where we are starting, where we intend to finish, and the environment we are in.

Bill Walsh, who won four Super Bowl titles as the coach of the San Francisco 49ers, was known for his innovative game plans and, above all, his thorough preparation. He authored a book titled, "The Score Takes Care of Itself: My Philosophy of Leadership." *The Score Takes Care of Itself?* What an amazing concept! In the world of professional football, where most coaches are eventually fired based on their win-loss record, here was a coach more focused on the *process* than the *outcome*. Let's take a lesson! Instead of concentrating on the trailing-edge indicators, let's emphasize preparation and the decision-making process, and trust that the best possible results will follow.

If we as Product Managers concentrate on the decision-making process – doing the right things, at the right time, for the right reasons – we can be confident we will get the best possible results. The score will take care of itself. And that is what Product Management success looks like.

But first, we must be well-versed in Product Management theory. First, we have to know the fundamentals.

Chapter 2
THE PRODUCT LIFECYCLE

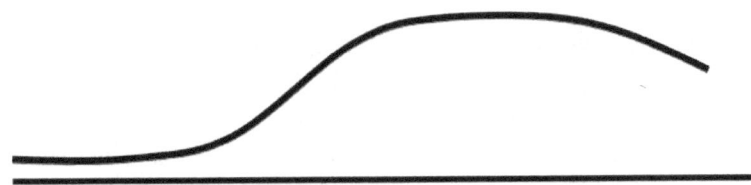

"If you don't like change, you're going to like irrelevance even less."
General Eric Shinseki

If the role of the Product Manager is to make the best possible decisions to drive the product lifecycle curve, we should begin with a brief discussion of the typical curve, and why it is the way it is.

The product lifecycle curve is simply the product Sales Revenue over time. It is a commercial-facing indicator that tells us how well our product is being accepted by the target customers, in the target market, at our price. If we think of the Value Prop as the compelling reason to buy the product at a particular price, then the lifecycle curve is actually a reflection of the *health* of our Value Prop.

Every product lifecycle curve is different, but many roughly follow the characteristic "S" curve as shown in Figure 2.1, with four phases:

- Launch: initial sales following introduction of the product to the market
- Growth: rapidly increasing sales and profit as the Value Prop gains traction
- Maturity: Revenue flattens as competitive alternatives erode the Value Prop and end our exclusivity
- Decline: decreasing Revenue as the Value Prop is no longer sustained

Figure 2.1   Typical Lifecycle Curve

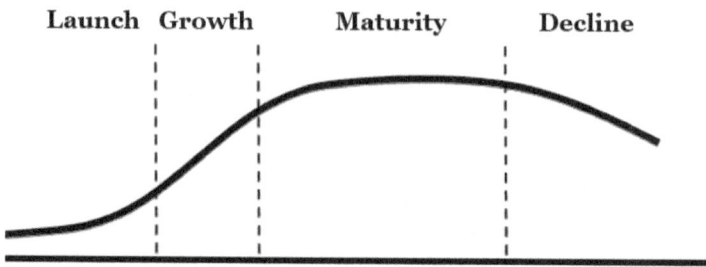

As an alternative to tracking Revenue over time, some companies prefer to track the volume of units sold. While this can be useful for a variety of reasons, especially for capacity planning, the disadvantage of doing this is it can mask the effects of price pressure and lead to some false indications about where the product is in the lifecycle. For example, if the company sells more units by dropping price, then the product may well be in the Mature phase, not the Growth phase. We will see an example later of a popular consumer product that experienced a volume peak one year after the Revenue peak. Correctly knowing the right phase is important for making the best decisions about investing for capacity, establishing inventory targets, setting pricing, executing the channel strategy, and other business-critical issues. While it is certainly useful to track unit volume, Revenue is the primary indication of product lifecycle phase.

It is also important to track profitability, such as Gross Margin over time, as this is a key indicator of how well the product is being managed holistically, since GM considers price, units and cost. As we will see, this actually becomes the bellwether financial metric in the Mature phase. However, this does not take the place of the Revenue-based lifecycle curve which speaks to the customer and market acceptance of the product.

Of course, not all product curves are alike. If a product has a highly intuitive Value Prop and a well-established ecosystem, adoption occurs sooner and the curve is effectively steeper. Alternatively, if the Value Prop is less intuitive, or the ecosystem requires considerable development, adoption is slower and the curve is less steep. The difference between these scenarios is the difference in the amount and timing of Revenue realization, which is why we will put considerable emphasis on fostering the ecosystem, educating the market, and creating intuitive Value Props when we talk about product Launch and Growth.

Figure 2.2   Impact of Value Prop and Ecosystem

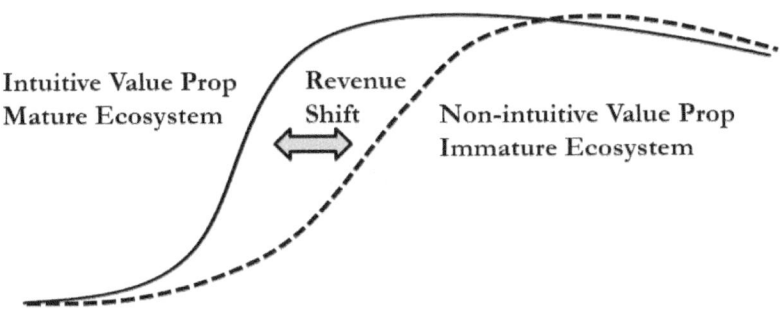

There are other distinctive product lifecycle curves as well. A product "fad," for example, would have a rapid rise and equally rapid fall, with a very short lifetime. In fashion, there might be multiple peaks as a particular "look" goes in and out of style. As we will discuss in the chapter on Maturity, it may be possible to reestablish a product preference or premium by introducing a distinguishing feature or attribute that again creates differentiation. This could effectively create a new Growth phase. Or, it may be possible to "spinoff" a niche variation of the product. The original product may continue to march toward Decline, while the niche product establishes a new lifecycle curve of its own.

Ultimately, it comes back to how well the Value Prop resonates with the market. To better understand the lifecycle curve, let's take a look at where good products – and good Value Props – come from.

Chapter 3
PRODUCT PLANNING AND THE VALUE PROP

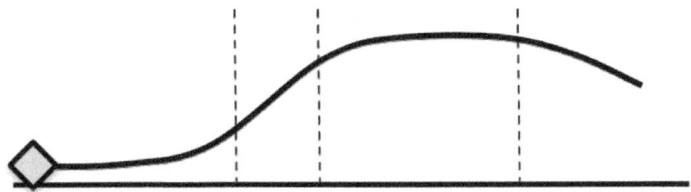

"If I had asked people what they wanted, they would have said faster horses." Henry Ford[1]

We introduced the term Value Prop in the previous chapter. This is a term many people are familiar with, but definitions tend to vary from person to person, and are typically not very rigorous. For many products, especially those sold in the Consumer space, what is referred to as the Value Prop is often a Marketing positioning statement that is designed to appeal to the user's experience. These frequently tend towards emotional superlatives as opposed to quantifiable benefits. The product is the fastest, the easiest, or the safest. It gets teeth their whitest, clothes their cleanest, or breath its freshest. Many are related to establishing and perpetuating the brand experience - - the look and feel that are associated with the product or the brand. This is important, but this is not what we mean here when we are talking about the Value Prop. As we have said, much of Product Management comes back to the Value Prop, and the shape of the Product Lifecycle curve is a reflection of the health of the Value Prop. So, for our purposes,

---

[1] Though this quote is widely attributed to Ford, there is some reason to doubt he actually made the statement. However, it does illustrate a common pitfall with VOC. https://hbr.org/2011/08/henry-ford-never-said-the-fast

we will use a very specific definition that directly connects our product solution to the customer problem in terms of three critical components.

The Value Prop is the *quantifiable benefit* of the product, from the *customer's perspective*, compared to the *next best alternative*. Each of these elements will be discussed in more detail later in this chapter.

The Value Prop is created and quantified during the Product Planning process when we identify solutions to specific customer problems. It then becomes an integral part of the product for both internal- and external-facing communications. Internally, the expected financial returns depend on the degree to which the product solves the customer's problem. The Value Prop drives the assumptions of price and customer adoption that fuel the Business Case and justify the allocation of resources for product development. It is also translated into compelling, external-facing Marketing position statements that clearly capture and communicate the benefit of the product to the customer. It is absolutely essential to get this right, so let's review the process that generates both our products and the Value Props that support them.

The Product Planning Process

A simplified Product Planning process is shown in Figure 3.1. Your company probably does something similar. You may use different terminology, but the fundamental concepts should be about the same. Let's review this process step by step.

Market Environment: Check the weather!

The current and future Market Environments have a critical influence on customer needs. As shown in Figure 3.1, the environment is a consideration throughout the entire Product Planning cycle, and even throughout the entire product lifecycle which follows. **The Market Environment never ceases to matter!** The environment may not only alter the customer's problems significantly, it will also impact the solution options we choose to offer. As we said, the Market Environment is like the weather. We cannot control the weather, but we may be able to forecast it, and we certainly should prepare for it!

Figure 3.1   Product Planning Process

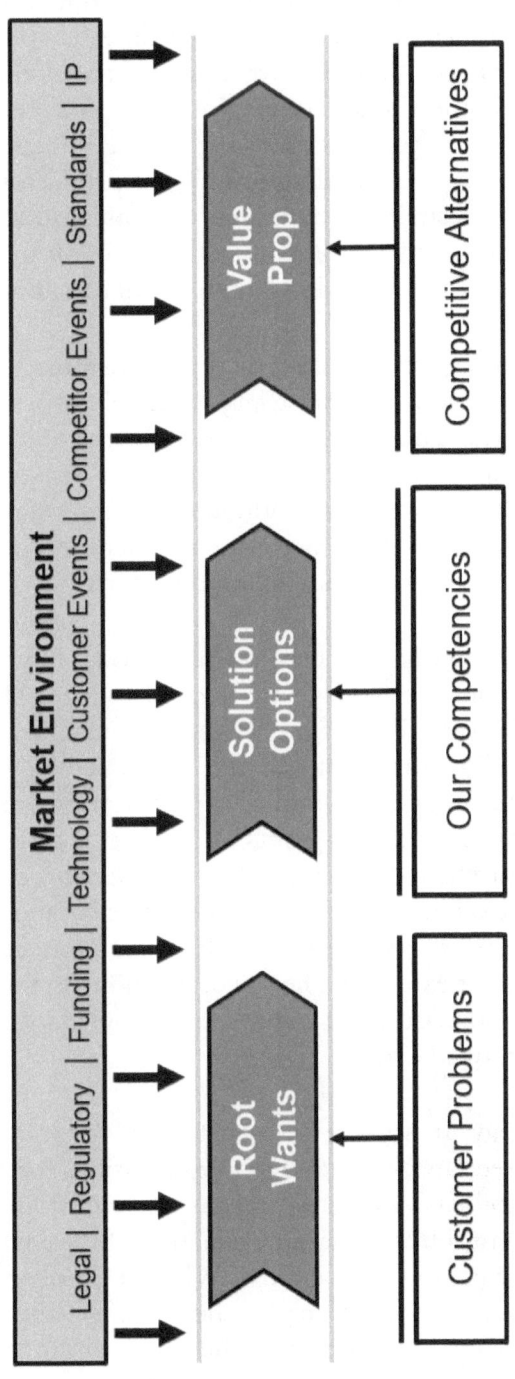

Like the weather, the Market Environment is constantly changing. It is important to consider not only the environment today, but also how the environment will change by the time our product is ready. Some customer needs may be further aggravated as the environment changes, while others may be mitigated or even eliminated. The environment can help our cause, such as a government stimulus program which provides funding to buy our product. Or, it can hurt us, such as trade restraints which limit our ability to sell our product overseas. To reasonably assess, forecast, and act on the environment, we should evaluate the following environmental factors:

- Legal and regulatory requirements: A customer (or competitor, for that matter) may be legally compelled to adapt to a new requirement. This can create new problems or change old ones. For example, new automobile emissions standards and safety requirements are typically announced long before they go into effect. How will these affect a customer's problem statement? How will they impact our solution options?

- Follow the money: It may seem obvious, but where will the customer get the money to buy our product? This is relatively straightforward if we are selling a consumer product, but considerably more complicated if we are selling to a business or a government agency. Is there a federal program that provides tax incentives, loans or grants? If so, is that program subject to significant change based on the next election cycle, or does it have a fixed termination date? Does the customer have a budget for buying our product? Is the sale of our product dependent on the customer extending their debt position? In this case, how far will they go? Are there indicators or triggers that will signal a change in this factor?

- Technology: It is no secret that technology moves quickly. As we will see later, technology is responsible for the demise of many products, as better means are developed for solving customer problems. For our evaluation of the environment, how could technology impact us? What technology changes are anticipated, and how might they change the environment? Moore's Law, for example, is the observation that the number of transistors on an integrated circuit board roughly doubles every two years. If your company competes in the consumer electronics arena, how do you incorporate this continuing evolution into your plans? How might the customer's problem statements change? How might this impact our solution options, or the competitor's plans?

- Customer and competitor plans: What changes are happening in the competitive landscape? Is there consolidation? Is someone exiting the business? Is someone entering a new market? Has there been an unfavorable legal judgement which limits a competitor's ability to compete? In 2019, the FCC issued a ban on the use of government funding to purchase equipment from Chinese telecom giant Huawei. Actions such as this fundamentally change the competitive landscape.

- Standards: Similar to legal requirements, industry standards may limit how, or if, a company can compete. They also drive product commoditization. What is happening with our industry standards? Do the industry standards allow for the products or attributes we are considering? Can we influence the standard? Is a customer influencing the standard? Is a competitor?

- Intellectual Property (IP): How does the IP landscape look? Is a key patent expiring, opening the door for increased competition? Are competitor filings limiting our solution options? Consider not only our own IP portfolio, but also customers' and competitors'.

When considering the upcoming weather forecast, we must evaluate it from three points of view: our customers' perspective, our own perspective, and our competitors' perspective. How are the customer's problems changing? What new problems might they have, and what opportunities will we have to solve them? If customers merge, if a standard is revised, if the technology advances, what does it mean to the customer's problems? What does it mean for our solutions? What does it mean for our competitors? And, knowing (or, at least, forecasting) these things, what will we do? How will we act differently? To paraphrase an oft-used mantra: No prizes for predicting rain; prizes only for building arks! We must understand the environment, assess the impact, and act appropriately.

Identify "Root Wants": What seems to be the problem here?

Our customers have problems. They have unmet needs. Ultimately, our product success ties directly back to their *Root Wants* and how well our products address them. Simply put, the Root Want is the customer's fundamental desire. What do they *really* want? We can win if we can provide solutions that solve their problems. So, the first step is deep understanding of what those problems are. How do we do this?

Well, we could try asking them. "Seek first to understand," as Stephen Covey puts it[2]. Gathering Voice of Customer (VOC) is necessary as part of any product definition, but be careful! The customers may presume solutions that are limited by their vision of what is possible, potentially sending us down the wrong path.

Early in my professional career, I worked providing customer support as an Applications Engineer. This included daily calls with customers who were either experiencing problems or seeking education and guidance on the field use of our products. One of the most valuable lessons I learned is that the customer rarely asked the "right" question initially. They almost never asked the thing they really wanted to know. Rather, they often presumed a solution to a problem they were experiencing, and asked about the feasibility of that solution. Giving them a direct answer to their question rarely resolved the issue. I learned to ask, "What problem are you having?" or, "What are you trying to do?" Many times, their initial question had little to do with their real concern.

VOC is an integral part of the equation, but our efforts must be focused on discovering the root problem before presuming any solutions. To accomplish this, there is no substitute for direct observation of what the customer is trying to do, and how their current options fail to deliver the Root Want. Product Managers must have a good understanding of how and where their product will be installed, handled, stored, and used. This understanding begins with experiencing the customer's situation first hand. Only then can we help the customer articulate the true Root Want.

But, even outside of dedicated VOC efforts, customers may already

---

[2] Stephen R. Covey, The 7 Habits of Highly Effective People

be telling us about their experiences. Are they entering field complaints? What are they telling our Sales agents? What are they telling Customer Service? What are they saying in Account reviews? Again, focusing on the problems they are having is key to determining a winning solution.

This step is critical! The "Root Wants" will drive the product requirements and form the basis for the Value Prop. We will be coming back to this customer and showing them how well our product solves their problem, so we better understand what that problem really is.

Develop Solution Options: Building (and selling) a better mousetrap

Once we have deep understanding of the customer's problems, we can explore our options for creating a solution. This is where we leverage our team of experts to translate our thorough understanding of the customer's Root Want into products that solve their problems. We want the product solution to be effective and efficient for the customer. After all, we intend to sell it to them. Here we should note that a "product" can take many different forms. It may be something tangible, like hardware or equipment, or something intangible, such as software or a service. It could also be a bundled solution comprised of many different elements, but always coming back to, "What problem are we solving?"

As we brainstorm possible solutions to the customer's problem, we also have to consider our own competencies and limitations, as well as those of the competitors. We not only want the solution to be effective for the customer, it needs to fit within our capabilities. And, we want it to be hard to displace. We will need barriers to future competitive offerings. These barriers are often in the form of IP, which can prohibit the competitors from copying key elements of our solution, but there are other effective barriers as well. What strengths do we have? What are our core competencies? Especially, what can we leverage that will be difficult for the competitors to overcome? Maybe it's technology, which puts the solution beyond their capability. Or, perhaps it is precision manufacturing, or supply chain logistics, or field engineering support. If the opportunity is large enough, we might even consider adding core competencies through hiring, partnering, or acquisitions.

Once solutions are identified, it is necessary to narrow the possibilities to the single best option. (In rare cases, parallel development of a couple of solutions may make sense.) The task of narrowing the options is a complicated undertaking which will not be presented here in detail. Suffice it to say the process should consider:

- The capabilities and limitations of our Technology team.
- The time, cost, and benefit of development v. other product development opportunities.
- The timing of product availability relative to the anticipated commercial window of an opportunity.
- The financial payback.
- Sustainability of the solution.
- Strategy fit.
- Corporate financial expectations and limitations.
- Confidence in our understanding of the market, customer, and problem.

Create the Value Prop: Establish the blueprint to win!

Let's review what we have accomplished to this point. First, we assessed the Market Environment to understand the forces that shape the competitive landscape and impact the customers. Next, we developed deep understanding of the customer's problems and Root Wants through VOC, direct observation, and other means. Then, we combined this thorough understanding of the Root Want with our core competencies and competitive advantages to identify and narrow the solution options. What we have now is a product concept that solves the customer's problem and matches our capabilities. Now, as we prepare to develop and launch this product, we must articulate the Value Prop.

The Value Prop is the ultimate output of the Product Planning exercise. The Value Prop demonstrates our understanding of the customer's fundamental problem – their Root Want – and clearly articulates how our product will solve the problem *better* than any existing or anticipated alternative. Our Value Prop will form the basis of customer-facing sales and marketing pitches, and it will also drive the underlying assumptions of the Business Case that will be used to prioritize this product development opportunity against competing projects. New products require development, which means resources must be justified based on financial payback. The Value Prop will provide the commercial assumptions that drive the Business Case, such as sales volume assumptions and price expectations.

Now, returning to our previous definition, the Value Prop is:
The *quantifiable benefit* of the product...
...from the *customer's perspective*...
...compared to the *next best alternative*

Quantifiable Benefit

We want to articulate the benefit with significant rigor and detail. While selling consumer products based on emotional reactions and user experience is often very effective, emotional superlatives don't go very far if we are selling our product in the business-to-business (B2B) space. We are unlikely to meet a Procurement Agent, an Engineer, or a Corporate Executive who will buy our product solely on our assertion that it is faster/easier/better. There will always be the same immediate follow-up question: *How much* faster, easier, or better? And so, in the B2B space especially, the benefit must be quantified. What's more, whenever possible, we want to dollarize the benefit to the customer. If our product is "faster", can we use a time savings and a labor rate to estimate the benefit, in dollars, to the customer? Can we dollarize the benefit of a product that is "more efficient"? If so, we can use the Value Prop to help develop our pricing strategy. A *quantified* Value Prop is essential; a *dollarized* Value Prop is ideal.

Customer's Perspective

It should be painfully obvious, but the Value Prop must articulate the benefit *from the viewpoint of the customer*. Both the emotional experience factor as well as the quantifiable benefit are lost if they are not from the perspective of the customer.

Next Best Alternative

When creating the Value Prop, we need to consider the customer's other options, especially the Next Best Alternative. This relates directly back to the Value Prop being from the *customer's perspective*. We have to ask the questions, "How would they solve the problem without our product? What other options do they have?" They may opt for a product from a competitor, or they may use a different technology, or they may implement a work-around to avoid the problem entirely. Here again, direct observation can provide unparalleled insight. Put yourself in your customer's shoes: what alternatives do you have? What would you do?

Finally, when assessing the Value Prop, we must understand the commercial situation is *dynamic*. We cannot assume that our competitors stand still. They are also identifying Root Wants and considering their own strengths and solution options. They are developing products as well. This means the Next Best Alternative can be a moving target, and our Value Prop can be eroded before we even finish development. Miss this point, and we may launch a product with no sustained commercial advantage. We'll see a painful example of this in Chapter 5.

To know our Value Prop *perfectly* means we know what the customer's problem is, how the problem is affecting them, and we know exactly how much better our product is at solving it than any other alternative. More specifically, we know *how to price* our product amid the competitive alternatives. When known perfectly, the "units" of the Value Prop are *dollars*.

Value Prop Examples

The Value Prop, as we have defined it, is an internal figure of merit, although it often directly drives the commercial positioning of the product. While we cannot know the precise Value Prop of a particular, real-life product, we can see how the product is positioned. Here are some examples of consumer products where the Value Prop is evident in the Marketing positioning.

Tankless Water Heaters

Tankless water heaters reduce energy consumption by heating water as it is needed, eliminating the cost of maintaining 50 or so gallons of hot water at all times. However, tankless water heaters carry a price premium, often $350 or more above the price of a conventional water heater. At least one manufacturer of tankless water heaters cites a study which determined a tankless gas water heater saves a family of four $95 per year, or $1,800 over its lifetime[3]. In this case, the benefit of \$95/year is clearly quantified from the customer's perspective, and is used to justify the price premium compared to a conventional water heater.

Smart Thermostats

Programmable "smart" thermostats lower utility costs through the use of scheduled heating and cooling, by detecting unoccupied rooms, and by "learning" the owner's preferences and behaviors. One of the leading manufacturers, Nest, cites a study demonstrating an average savings of \$131 to \$145 a year. With a typical price tag of \$250 or less, Nest suggests a payback period of less than two years for homeowners who upgrade from a conventional thermostat[4].

High-efficiency HVAC Filters

Home HVAC systems require filters to eliminate dust, pet hair, and other particles. A basic 3M Filtrete™ filter which eliminates lint and household dust is available at a major US retailer for about \$3. Alternatively, 3M also offers Filtrete filters with the additional benefit of eliminating allergens, such as smog, smoke and pollen. These high-efficiency filters are available at the same retailer at roughly 4x the price of the basic unit. We can interpret this price difference as the value to the customer of the anti-allergen feature.

NOTE: For simplicity, these examples focus on different products as opposed to different brands. In reality, a company like Nest must consider not only their differences v. conventional thermostats, but also their differences v. other makers of smart thermostats.

---

[3] *Save Money and More with ENERGY STAR Qualified Whole-Home Gas Tankless Water Heaters,*
https://www.energystar.gov/products/water_heaters/water_heater_whole_home_gas_tankless/benefits_savings

[4] 'Energy Savings from the Nest Learning Thermostat: Energy Bill Analysis Results', p. 6, https://storage.googleapis.com/nest-public-downloads/press/documents/energy-savings-white-paper.pdf

Compendium

- The current and future Market Environments have a significant impact on the Product Planning process and throughout the product lifecycle.
- Key elements of the Market Environment include legal and regulatory requirements, sources of funding, technology, and changes in the customer and competitor landscape.
- Deep understanding of the customer's problem through direct observation and VOC enables us to clearly define Root Wants.
- Combining the customer's Root Wants with our core competencies allows us to identify solution options that could be developed and offered.
- Evaluating our solution options against current and future competitive alternatives allows us to articulate a meaningful Value Prop.
- The Value Prop is defined as the *quantifiable benefit* of the product, from the *customer's perspective*, compared to the *next best alternative.*
- When known perfectly, the Value Prop is dollarized and defines the maximum price premium we could potentially achieve.
- A quantifiable Value Prop is used to drive the Business Case assumptions that will enable internal project prioritization, as well as to create compelling customer talking points.

Chapter 4
THE LIFECYCLE EXAMPLE EVERYONE KNOWS[5]

"Every new beginning comes from some other beginning's end."
Seneca, Roman Philosopher

As we have discussed, the product lifecycle curve is an indication of the viability of the Value Prop, and the Value Prop, in turn, captures the extent to which the product and its attributes satisfy the Root Wants of the customer. What problem is our product solving, and how well? Let's consider one example of a Root Want, and the evolution of products and technology that have sought to meet that need with ever-improving Value Props.

It's probably fair to say there is a Root Want for music on demand: the ability to hear the artists and songs you like, when and where you want to hear them. Since music has been around for a long, long time, it is also probably fair to say this Root Want has always existed. People may not have been able to clearly articulate this desire 100+ years ago because they were confined by the limits of their imagination. They simply could not conceive of the world of streaming music services of the 21st century, but suffice it to say the *want* was always there.

---

[5] All music sales data courtesy of the Recording Industry Association of America and reproduced with permission. Values in Billion USD and inflation adjusted to 2019. US market only. https://www.riaa.com/u-s-sales-database/

As Product Managers, understanding the fundamental Root Want, could we have anticipated where this was headed? Could we have made good decisions about what was coming? What can we learn?

Let's review.

Pre-1973: Edison's Phonograph

The phonograph was invented in 1877 by Thomas Edison as a means of recording sound. In the 1890s, Emile Berliner modified Edison's invention by changing the recording medium from cylinders to flat discs. This led eventually to the widely popular vinyl record as a medium for distributing recorded music, and the first iteration of music "on demand" was born. By the 1970s, vinyl records were well-established because of their faithful sound reproduction, wide availability, mature ecosystem, and reasonable price.

This is not to say that vinyl albums fully satisfied the Root Want. Sound quality could be adversely affected by a dirty stylus or worn album. Vinyl records might become warped by heat, or mechanically scratched, causing them to "skip" when played. But, even in a pristine state, vinyl albums had an inherent shortcoming: the music was not really portable. You could not bring your favorite music with you to the beach, on a walk, or in your car. In terms of satisfying the Root Want of music on demand, they still left a lot to be desired. Although vinyl was the best alternative of the time, technology would soon change things.

1973-1983: Magnetic Tape and the Unintended Consequence

Along came magnetic tape as an alternative medium for recording audio. Once the tape packaging was standardized, primarily in the form of cassettes and 8-tracks, a competitor to vinyl records was available. By the early 1970s, technological advancements in the form of chromium oxide tape and Dolby® noise reduction gave cassette tapes comparable sound quality to vinyl. And, cassettes and 8-tracks made the music portable. Tape players became commonplace in cars and homes. In 1979, Sony released the Walkman®, taking portable, personal music to a new level. With comparable sound quality, a smaller form factor, and easy portability, cassettes and 8-tracks were poised to replace vinyl as the medium of choice. They simply had a better Value Prop.

Except that didn't happen.

Figure 4.1   US Music Sales by Format, 1973-1983, $Billion

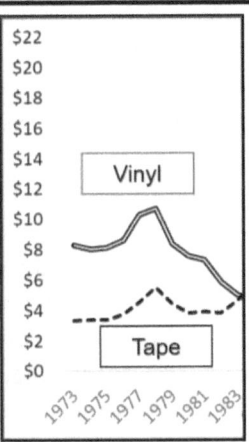

Figure 4.1 is a graph of prerecorded music sales on vinyl and tape (all forms) in the US, from 1973 to 1983. As seen in the graph, tape sales remained relatively consistent at roughly half the sales of vinyl for most of this period. Perhaps more surprising, following a brief spike in demand in 1977-78, overall sales of prerecorded music actually began to decline. The market, it seemed, was shrinking. While tape sales remained more or less flat throughout the period, vinyl album sales were clearly declining after 1978. Five years later, in 1983, tape sales finally exceeded vinyl sales, but this had more to do with declining vinyl sales as opposed to a great surge in demand for tape. This is certainly not what we would expect, especially with the recent improvement in music portability provided by cassettes and 8-tracks. Customers were offered additional choices, which better satisfied the Root Want, and the market...*declined?* What in the world was going on?

One thing to remember is the graph shown is sales of prerecorded music. Instead of being purely competing technologies, tape and vinyl actually formed somewhat of a collaborative relationship. Many customers continued to buy albums, then also bought *blank* cassette tapes and *copied* the albums for use in their cars and other portable music devices. What's more, prospective customers were borrowing vinyl albums from their friends to dub onto blank cassettes. As a result, one album sale might result in multiple tape copies. More music was in circulation, but prerecorded music sales were lower. Although this practice violated copyright protection, there was little to no chance of stopping it.

In addition, the practice of dubbing albums also enabled the user to create a custom tape. Maybe it was their own version of a "greatest hits", or simply a recording that left out songs they didn't like, or maybe the ever-popular "mix tape" of various songs and artists. After all, isn't this more in line with the Root Want of having just the music you like?

Now perhaps the graph makes more sense. Since the vinyl album came first, that ecosystem was already established. The invention of magnetic cassette tapes with excellent sound quality cannibalized a portion of the vinyl demand, but the primary consumer benefit was the ability to *copy* albums. Since multiple tapes were being created from a single album, the market for prerecorded music began to decline. At a time when music was expanding in popularity, the market size as measured in dollars was actually shrinking. Piracy was largely to blame for the decline, and it had been enabled by the advancement of the cassette tape. This was a problem for the music industry that would recur a few years later.

1983-2000: Digital Technology Drives the Market

The first commercial releases of music on compact disc came in 1982. Now here was a superior Value Prop! CDs (and music DVDs) offered significantly improved fidelity over either albums or tape. They were portable. They were more rugged than vinyl with a size roughly comparable to tape. Rapid advances in technology enabled multi-disc players and portable devices. CDs were simply a better technology for delivering music on demand than anything that came before them.

But, early adoption of CDs was hampered by the ecosystem. That is, nobody initially had CD players, especially in their cars. The earliest deployment of CD players in commercial automobiles did not begin until 1985, and widespread adoption did not occur for another ten years. Also, early units were susceptible to skipping due to mechanical vibration, especially on rough roads, and there was some skepticism about whether or not the improved sound quality could be appreciated with wind and road noise. Still, the inherently superior Value Prop of the CD led to almost immediate displacement of vinyl.

Figure 4.2   US Music Sales by Format, 1973-1999, $Billion

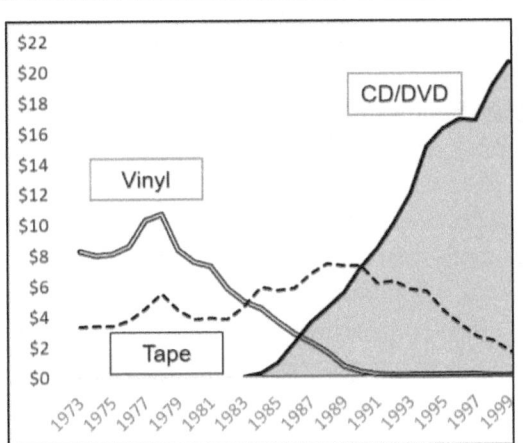

By 1987, CD sales already surpassed record sales in the US. The cassette tape hung on a little longer, and even saw a decade of increased sales from 1984 to 1994. This, again, is attributable to the ecosystem. Since music portability was a primary market driver, and most cars already on the road had cassette players but not CD players, the cassette survived for a time. However, with more and more new cars equipped with CD players, sales of cassette and 8-track music began to fall in the early 1990s. There was no denying that compact discs had a superior Value Prop when it came to addressing the Root Want of music on demand. By 1991, music sales on CD exceeded tape sales, and vinyl was all but dead. By 2000, CD sales totaled $20B, accounting for 95% of the market. Other than some niche sales of vinyl albums, the superior Value Prop of CDs had literally driven tape and vinyl into extinction.

Looks like the game is over. Or is it?

2000-2011: Personal Computing and The Rise of Napster®

In the early 21st century, personal computing began to explode. Since the CD format was useful for storing large quantities of data, not just music, CD read-write drives came to be standard on PCs. This extension of the CD ecosystem ironically facilitated the instrument of the CD's demise as a prerecorded music medium. In June of 1999, just as PC usage was becoming widespread, Napster was launched as a Peer-to-Peer (P2P) file sharing service. Especially popular with

Napster users was the ability to exchange audio files in an MP3 format over the internet. Just as customers had borrowed vinyl albums from friends to dub onto cassettes, now they could exchange MP3 files with virtually anyone. Everyone using the file share service suddenly became your friend. Chances are, someone had the album you wanted, and participants could download the album or songs, burn them to a CD, and get the music they wanted in the format they wanted at virtually no cost.

However, these copyright violations were more blatant and addressable than their predecessors. Napster quickly ran into legal trouble and, by 2001, the service was shut down. However, the business model was now readily apparent. Instead of selling records, cassettes or CDs through high-overhead retail outlets, there was an opportunity to sell music as downloadable files from a central repository. It was no coincidence when, on January 9, 2001, iTunes® was launched by Apple. This was another leap toward delivering the fundamental Root Want. MP3 players began to grow in popularity. Now users could legally download and pay for only the music they wanted and put it onto small, portable players with *no physical media*.

Figure 4.3   US Music Sales by Format, 1973-2011, $Billion

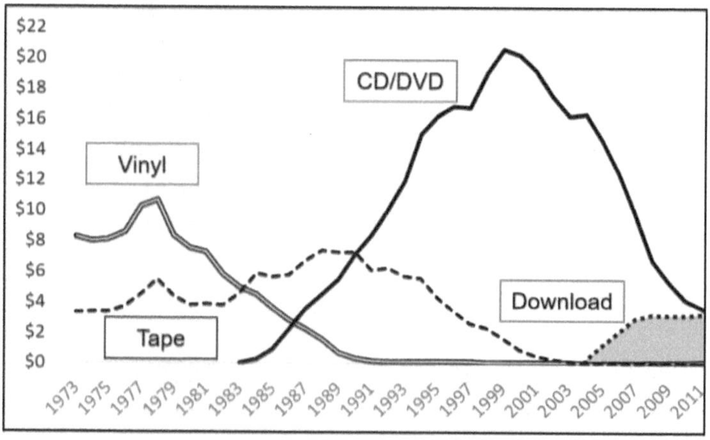

Talk about a game changer! Sales of downloaded music grew and drove CDs and music DVDs quickly towards end-of-life. Also, as sales shifted toward individual songs and away from entire albums, the overall market further declined. Just as CDs had systematically killed vinyl and tape with a superior Value Prop, digital downloads pushed CDs off a cliff. The CD technology that brought so much value in terms of sound quality, portability, form factor, and music on demand, had come and gone in a period of about 30 years.

2011-2019: Streaming Overtakes Everything

It might seem that downloading digital music would be the end of the line for the evolution of music media. Going back to the Root Want, aren't we there now? Get just the songs you like, play them in any order you like. Load them on your phone and take them with you anywhere with no physical media. Connect your phone wirelessly in your car, or to a speaker, or to earphones. Music on demand? Mission accomplished.

Almost.

We still only have the songs we buy. How do we address a 'try it before you buy it' desire? A band you like has put out an album. You like the new single, the only one they play on the radio, so you pay to download it. What about the rest of the album? You might like it as well, but then again, you might not. It would be nice to give it a listen before you pay to download it.

Or, how do you feel about paying to load up your phone with songs you liked for a while, but never listen to anymore?

What people really wanted was the ability to listen to literally any song, at any time, in any place. Isn't that what music on demand is all about? Well, someone figured all that out. And how to deliver it. Streaming music services first began to emerge around 2005, and by 2012 annual sales topped $1B. 2012 was also the year that sales of downloaded digital music peaked. After this, streaming services continued to gather steam, began to grow, and pushed all other music formats to niche status.

Figure 4.4   US Music Sales by Format, 1973-2019, $Billion

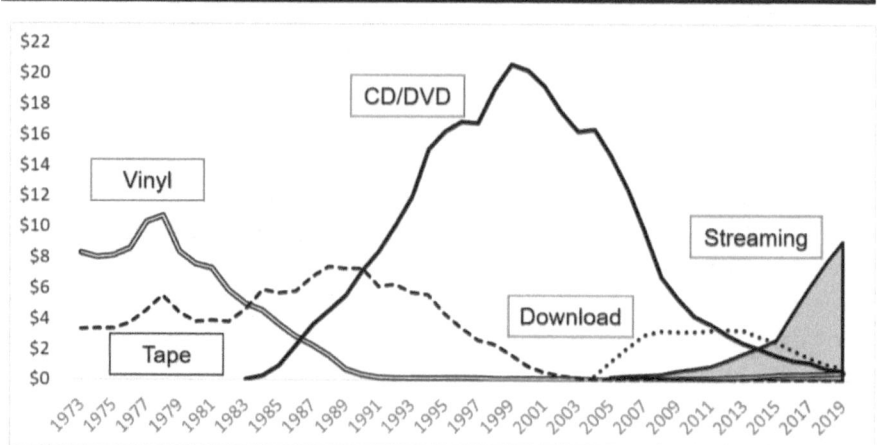

Industry Impact

While all of this has been great for the consumer, it has not been so good for the music industry. It seems that the market has – again – shrunk.

Figure 4.5   US Music Market by Format, 1973-2019, $Billion

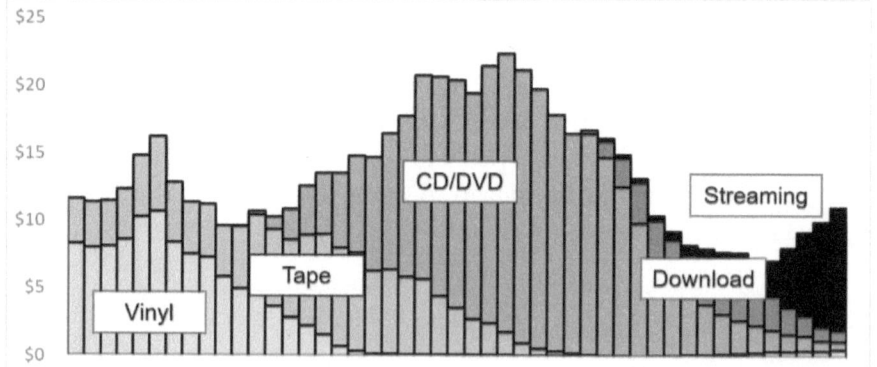

If we combine the sales of all music formats, we can generate the market graph in Figure 4.5. From a sales perspective, the music market clearly peaked at about $20B in 1999, nearly all of which was sales of

CDs and music DVDs. Piracy via P2P file sharing services initially eroded this peak, then legal download services continued the trend. Today, streaming services have replaced album sales, and competition among these services has left the market highly commoditized, leading to lower prices and a smaller total market. As indicated in Figure 4.5, after adjusting for inflation, the total market is roughly where it was in 1973.

Lessons Learned: What can we take away from this?
- The Root Want ultimately determines the winner in the market. Understand the real problem we are trying to solve. Music formats were systematically made obsolete by technologies that better satisfied the Root Want.
- Consider possible unintended consequences. Did anyone foresee the primary market for cassette tapes would be blank cassettes for dubbing albums, and not prerecorded music? Did anyone foresee advancements in tape technology would lead to *decreased* music sales?
- The ecosystem is critical. Initial CD adoption was impacted by the lack of CD players in cars.
- Look ahead. Sales of CDs peaked in 1999. Everything looked great, but trees don't grow to the sky! The demise of this product was already there as demonstrated by Napster and other P2P services.
- Pay attention to market forces and adjacencies. The incorporation of CD drives in home computers changed the ecosystem and the playing field.

Compendium

- Music on demand has always been a Root Want for consumers.
- The portability benefit of tape as a medium was not enough to displace vinyl sales as many consumers copied albums to blank audio tape, causing the overall market to shrink in the process.
- The Compact Disc offered a significantly more compelling Value Prop compared to vinyl and tape, and completely displaced these media forms once the ecosystem was established, especially factory-installed car CD players.
- Digital music downloads from iTunes and other sources eliminated the physical medium for music, leading to the demise of CDs.
- Streaming music services offer true on-demand music, fulfilling the original Root Want better than any preceding technology.

Chapter 5
THE BEGINNING (AND END) OF THE ZUNE®

"Good is not good when better is expected." Vin Scully

Before we get to the nuts and bolts of lifecycle management, let's consider another example from the world of music to illustrate the importance of sustaining the Value Prop. As previously noted, iTunes was launched in January 2001, ushering in a legitimate digital music service on the heels of P2P file sharing from Napster and similar websites. Digital music was inherently advantaged compared to CDs, tape, or vinyl, because there was no physical medium at all. What was initially lacking, however, was a mature ecosystem. What was lacking was a dominant digital music player. And that brings us to the Microsoft Zune. Not immediately, of course. The Zune would come – and go – in time, and is a worthwhile example of the importance of sustaining differentiation.

The Early Days of i-everything[6]

Let's review the world of digital music players in the early 21st century. Following the launch of iTunes in January 2001, Apple released the first iPod® in October of the same year. They introduced

---

[6]Philip Michaels, 'Timeline: iPodding through the years', *Macworld*
https://www.macworld.com/article/1053499/ipodtimeline.html

Figure 5.1   Digital Music Player Timeline

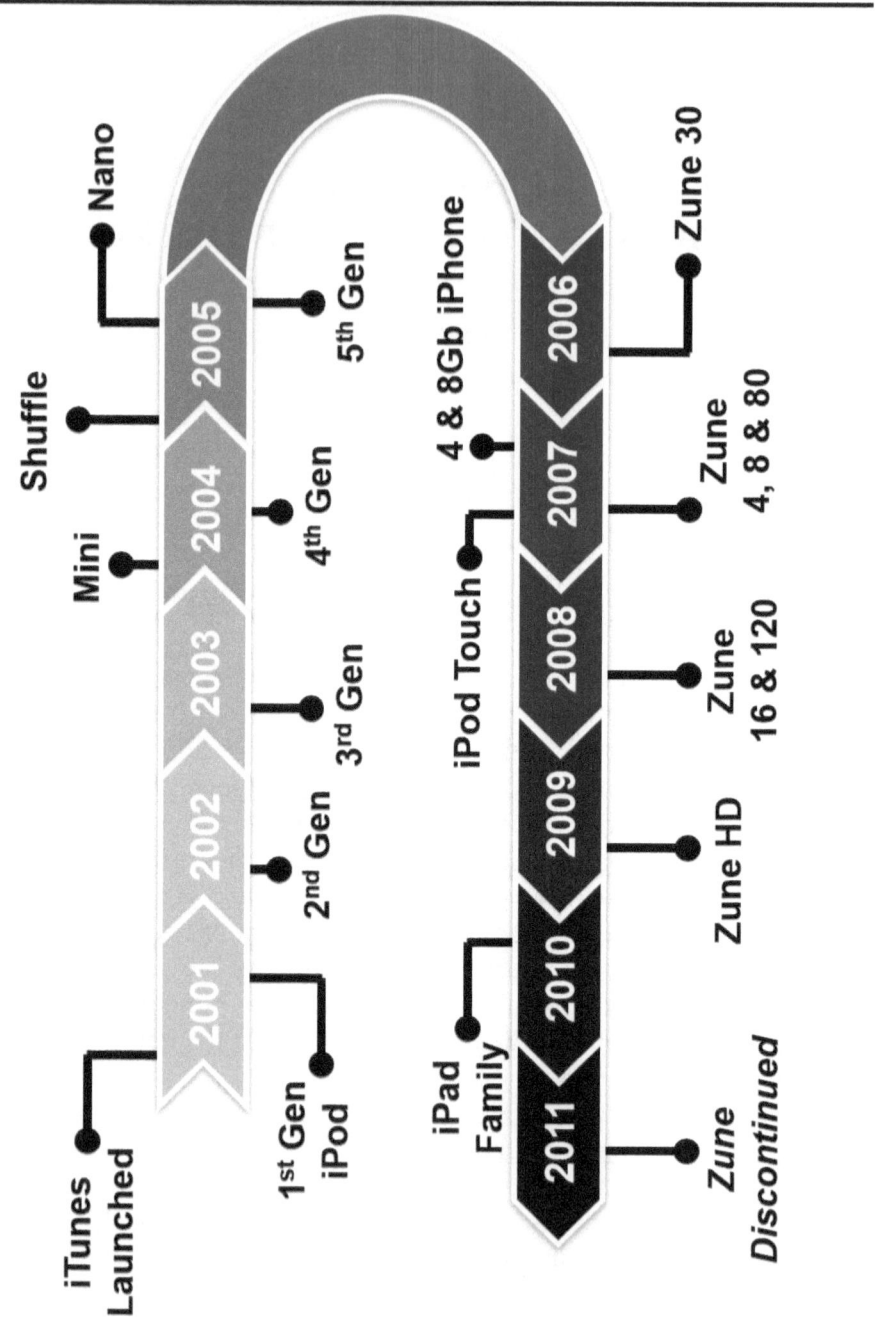

the 2nd generation iPod in 2002, and new generations continued to hit the market roughly every year. In January 2004, Apple added a more compact version, the iPod Mini, to the product portfolio. A year later, in January 2005, the iPod shuffle® was released. The iPod shuffle was the smallest of the iPod family, and the first to use flash memory. Another version with flash memory, the iPod nano®, came in September of 2005 as a replacement for the Mini.

Apple's product portfolio was continually evolving and improving. By the end of 2006, the 5th generation iPod was available, and the Nano and Shuffle were each on their 2nd generation. Along with these player enhancements, a myriad of ancillary devices and user apps had been developed and released into the ecosystem. The iPod touch® was less than a year away. Apple was the clear leader in the digital music hardware market.

And that is where the story of the Zune begins.

The Market Tipping Point and the New Competitor

Despite Apple's broad and growing product portfolio, the market for digital music was still relatively small in the early 2000s. Through 2004, Apple had sold fewer than 6M iPods, and the cumulative sale of downloaded music in the US totaled less than $250M. Neither product – the iPod nor downloaded music – had hit the Growth phase of the lifecycle. In 2005, the Value Prop hit a tipping point. Downloaded music sales reached $1.2B. iPod sales exceeded 22M units, roughly 4x the total cumulative sales prior to 2005, and accounting for more than 30% of Apple's 2005 Revenue. In 2006, Apple sold 39M iPods, again exceeding the historical total, and accounting for 40% of their annual sales. The sale of downloaded music topped $2B. When the market finally arrived, it *arrived.*

Encouraged by this trend, Microsoft elected to enter the market in November 2006 with their own digital media player, the Zune 30. Competing with Apple was nothing new to Microsoft, and they were certainly well-versed in launching new products. But, given the 5-year head start of the iPod product line, Microsoft had to consider and make choices about product features, the ecosystem, and, of course, price. They had to determine how they could *differentiate.* Now, it is worth noting that digital media players were not solely intended for playing music. They also incorporated screens for viewing pictures and, increasingly, videos. As Microsoft evaluated product features and price, they had to consider more than just the customer Root Wants as they pertained to music. They also had to consider customer Root Wants as they pertained to video playback experience.

Microsoft elected to design the Zune as a competitive alternative to the incumbent Gen 5 iPod, the industry leader at the time. The Zune 30 incorporated a 30Gb hard drive, matching the lower-end version of the iPod, which was being sold with both 30 and 60Gb options. The Zune also matched the screen resolution of the iPod. Differentiation came in the form of a larger screen size for the Zune (3.0" v. 2.5"). Although the larger screen contributed to the Zune being bigger and heavier than the iPod, it seemed better suited for satisfying the video preferences of the customers. Microsoft had elected to differentiate on the video experience. Combined with a simple user interface and the typical high-quality standards of a Microsoft product, the Zune seemed to be a worthy competitor in the space. Microsoft priced the units at $249, below the $299 price tag of the Gen 5 iPod.

Even in hindsight, it seems like a solid approach. What the Zune gave up with larger size and weight, it made up for with a larger screen and lower price. Six months after launch, the Zune had already garnered 10% of the hard drive digital media player market.

So, what happened?

Apple Continues to Innovate

What the Zune did not have was sustainable differentiation. In September 2007, just 10 months after the release of the Zune 30, Apple released the iPod touch. The iPod touch was considerably smaller and lighter than the Zune, and incorporated a larger (3.5" v. 3.0"), higher resolution touch screen, negating the Zune's previous advantage in video playback. The technology momentum built by Apple's 5-year head start proved to be too much. The Zune now seemed like a clunky, cumbersome, undifferentiated dinosaur compared to the smaller, sleeker Apple products. What's more, the Apple ecosystem had continued to grow. The Apple products were readily available with a broad range of accessories.

Going back to our music media example, the "unmet need" or "Root Want" is for music on demand: what you want to hear, when and where you want to hear it. The Zune might deliver this *as well* as the iPod, but *no better*. And, once Apple overcame the video advantage of the Zune, the Microsoft product had no clear differentiation. The (initially) larger screen gave Zune a brief advantage with video experience, but this was not long-lived. The iPod touch had advantages in screen size, screen resolution, weight, and overall size. And, it had a touchscreen. And, it was just cooler. The Zune began to look like what it was: a "me too" product launched into a market that was already dominated by a strong Tier 1 competitor who had significant first-mover advantage.

Robbie Bach, former leader of Microsoft's home entertainment and mobile business, summarized the demise of Zune by saying, "…we ended up chasing Apple with a product that actually wasn't a bad product, but it was still a chasing product, and there wasn't a reason for somebody to say, oh, I have to go out and get that thing."[7]

Apple never relinquished their lead in this space. In June 2007, the first iPhone® was released, which would eventually replace the iPod for music and video. In 2010, iPhone sales exceeded iPod sales for the first time.

In March 2011, Microsoft announced that no new Zune hardware players would be developed.

---

[7] Matt Rosoff, 'Former Microsoft Zune Boss Explains Why It Flopped', *Business Insider,* https://www.businessinsider.com/robbie-bach-explains-why-the-zune-flopped-2012-5

Compendium:

- Microsoft launched the Zune late into a market with a clear, established leader.
- The ecosystem of iPod accessories was already well established by the time Zune was introduced.
- Microsoft initially sought to differentiate the Zune based on the video experience by incorporating a larger screen size.
- Apple's technology advantage precluded Microsoft from establishing sustainable differentiation. By the time Zune was released, the iPod touch, iPad®, and the first iPhone were on their way, trampling the weak Zune Value Prop.

Chapter 6
LAUNCH

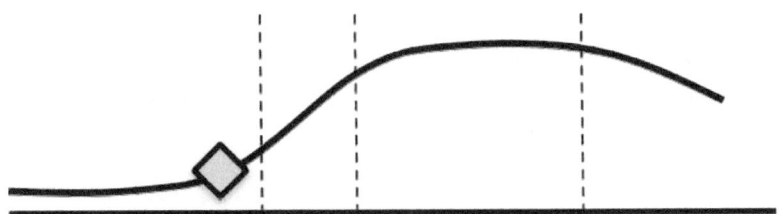

"Everybody has a plan until they get punched in the face."
Mike Tyson

I have interviewed a number of prospective Product Management candidates over the years. One of the questions I like to ask is, "Which is more important: planning or execution?" Most candidates proceed to explain the purpose and key elements of each, with the inevitable conclusion *both* are vitally important.

This is true, of course, but no one gets off that easily in a job interview. So, if you HAD to choose, is it better to be really good at planning, or really good at executing? There isn't a single right answer to this, but there are good answers that demonstrate an understanding of how planning and execution not only matter, but are interrelated to one another. One candidate correctly noted that a thorough, well-thought-out plan is one that is easily executed. Plan well, and the execution will follow. The rationale for the importance of good execution is even more straightforward: no matter how good your plan is, you can never foresee every obstacle or contingency. Something will always come up; something will always go wrong. Moreover, while excellent execution can sometimes overcome poor planning, the opposite is rarely true. Even the best plan can't overcome poor execution.

The whole point of the question, from a Product Management perspective, is related to product Launch. We typically get one good opportunity to launch a new product. Botch that, and the recovery will be painful and costly. Imagine that the product is launched, but customers can't order it because our systems aren't ready, or the product has unforeseen quality or performance issues, or the distribution network isn't in place, or the product literature is incorrect or unavailable. The damage could include a Sales force that loses confidence in the product, customers who lose patience with the rollout, and field or quality failures that carry both financial liability and lost customer trust. Instead of reaping the benefits of solving a customer problem, we are working double-time on corrective actions. Or, imagine that we fail to create a solid IP position. We could miss the soaring sales and profits of the Growth phase because we failed to create barriers to entry.

As the saying goes, you only get one chance to make a good first impression!

Planning and execution go hand-in-hand. A good plan facilitates simpler and more successful execution, while excellent execution can help overcome the inevitable shortcomings of the plan. Product Launch consists of thorough, comprehensive planning, followed by violent execution of the plan, with prompt response to the market reaction.

It should also be emphasized that Launch is an integrated event involving many, many parts of the organization, making the planning phase highly iterative. We may prefer to launch our product with a big splash announcement, making it available to all customers at the same time as part of a "digital" release. However, other factors, such as machine capacity, or the ecosystem, or the IP landscape, may drive us to a phased release, segmenting the customers by size, or importance, or region, or some other demographic. The capabilities and limitations of the organization and the market must be considered as part of the Launch. And so, we begin by talking about the Launch plan.

Pre-Launch Planning

Consider what is happening in the Launch phase. The product is introduced to customers, and sales begin once the Value Prop gains traction. We expect to be launching into an environment where there is an unmet need in the market for one or more customers. This, after all, is the whole premise of our Value Prop. But, if the product is solving an unmet need, that also means there is initially no market or customer awareness of it. Commercial education is required. Similarly, our own organization needs to be prepared. From Sales, to commercial and technical support, to Finance, to Manufacturing, organizational readiness is critical. What's more, our product development, manufacturing capacity, and commercial rollout must all be harmonized.

It is worth noting that many, or even most, aspects of the Launch phase are owned by organizations *other than* the Product Manager. However, if any aspect of the Launch goes poorly, it will be reflected in our P&L. As the owners of profitability, we live with the results. Product Managers must exert organizational leadership by influencing the groups that own each workstream!

Note: a suggested Launch checklist appears in Figure 6.2 at the end of this chapter.

Assess the Ecosystem

Our product will not exist in a vacuum. No doubt there are related or ancillary products that must work with it. Do these already exist? Are they available, and is the integration seamless? Does our product work with existing tools and established practices and protocols? Consider, for example, that the gasoline nozzle always fits in your car, or the lamp you buy today will plug into your existing wall socket, or even that your new smart phone or laptop will connect seamlessly to Wi-Fi networks in your home, in hotel rooms, or at a local coffee shop. We often take these things for granted because these are commodity products, and commoditization brings standardization. However, if you have travelled internationally, you know this is not always the case. Europe has different electrical standards from the US. The European and US electrical *ecosystems* are different. Industry standards are integral in facilitating the development of the ecosystem, but these standards may not consider our new product. Or, the necessary standards may not exist at all. In fact, if our product is truly addressing an unmet customer need, it is likely novel, and by definition, different. Pre-launch planning must include an assessment of the products, tools, procedures, and other items that will be commonly used with our new product.

Several years ago, during a period of low gasoline prices, US automakers introduced enormous sport utility vehicles (SUVs) targeted for sale to suburban families. Ford's flagship entrant in this arena was the Excursion. At nearly 19 ft long, up to 6'8" tall, and over 7,200 lbs., the Excursion was the longest and heaviest vehicle ever mass produced for the North American market[8]. One of the problems that became obvious after the product Launch was, the Excursion did not fit inside a standard size garage. The vehicle was incompatible with the ecosystem of the target demographic group, and this almost certainly contributed to its short lifespan. Following the 1999 introduction, sales quickly peaked in 2000 at over 50,000 units, then declined every year until Ford discontinued the behemoth in 2005, when only 16,000 vehicles were sold[9]. Though not the only reason for the demise of the Excursion, it certainly did not help that the vehicle failed to seamlessly integrate with the ecosystem of the targeted demographic group. While Ford did not control the ecosystem in this case, Executives and Product Managers should have been aware of this conflict well before Launch, and the impact it could have on the viability of the product.

As we prepare to launch our product, we need a thorough understanding of the ecosystem. Is it ready to support us? If not, what actions can we take? How can we control or influence it?

Cultivate the Commercial Environment

Hand-in-hand with the ecosystem is the commercial environment. Customers need to know about our product. They need to know how to use it, where to find it, how big it is, how much power it uses. Back to the Value Prop, they need to know why to buy it and what problem it solves. More fundamentally, they need to know that it even exists. Market awareness of the product must be cultivated as part of the Launch process.

1. Create Customer Positioning Statements: The Value Prop we created as part of Product Planning forms the basis for our customer communications. As we plan for our Launch, we must translate the Value Prop into focused customer positioning statements. A positioning statement is not a long list of features

[8] Dan McCosh, ed. 'Big, Bigger, Biggest', *Popular Science*, Nov 1999, p48
[9] *CARSALESBASE*, https://carsalesbase.com/us-ford-excursion/

and attributes, but rather should target the one or two critical benefits that particularly appeal to a specific customer persona. Bombarding the customer with a plethora of improvements or benefits only serves to *distract* from the problem being solved. Remaining focused keeps the message simple and the customer engaged. As we discussed previously, the value should be clearly quantified, and whenever possible, dollarized in the positioning statements.

As mentioned, the statements must also be relevant to the specific customer persona. That is, we may need to customize separate positioning statements for our conversations with Procurement, or with Engineering, or with Executives. For example, if the product is smaller and lighter, the positioning statement for Procurement might focus on reduced transportation costs, while the statement for Engineering might focus on easier installation or improved reliability, while the statement for the Executive might focus on the total improvement to the overall business.

2. Develop the Product Promotional Plan: How will the customers know about our product? Will the product be launched at an industry trade show? In this case, the timing of development and manufacturing capability must be anchored to this date. Or, will we approach customers one at a time to segment the Launch and mitigate the risk of demand uncertainty? Where and how will we advertise? The answers will vary widely depending on the product and the targeted market demographic, but our Promotional Plan must match our Launch strategy!

3. Anticipate the Customer Approval Process: Before we talk with customers about the product, we should anticipate their product approval requirements so we can incorporate the "answers" into our customer training plans. Whose approval is required? Will the customer require test data or certification? Testing might include safety, performance, lifetime, environmental impact, or other considerations. The requirement might be that we submit our own test data, or third-party certification might be required, or they may even want to evaluate the product in their own laboratory. Are they likely to require a field trial as part of the

approval process? Any of these can place significant constraints on our timeline, in part because we do not always control the scheduling of the testing, and we cannot dictate the approval process. Further, the possibility of a test failure creates additional risk to the plan. It is important to understand the approval process, identify the associated risks, and create a plan that includes contingencies.

4. Create the Customer Training Plan: Having considered the previous items, we now need a customer training plan to improve awareness and understanding of the product. Similar to the positioning statements, this training plan should be tailored to each targeted persona, but is much more in-depth. Purchasing needs to know how to order the product; Supply Chain needs to know how to track inventory; the field needs to know how and where the product is used and what is different about it. Training requires time, resources, and a carefully thought-out message. It also requires product collateral.

5. Develop Product Collateral: We need collateral to support the use of our product by the customers. This typically includes updated catalogs, product spec sheets, installation and handling procedures, and instructions for use. In addition, we need pertinent safety precautions and guidance on environmental considerations, such as proper product disposal or limitations on use. Increasingly, the collateral should be available in multiple formats, including both printed and electronic versions. The key is to *make it easy* for the customer to use our product. Who needs to see the collateral, and where will they be when they need it? This could mean a laminated sheet that ships with the product, or permanent labeling incorporated into the product itself, or a QR code that links to a video. We must ask ourselves, "What information does the customer need, and what are the best formats to provide it?"

Worth noting, consider which languages are needed for the product collateral. If you have recently purchased any products that require assembly, you may have noted the instructions increasingly rely on pictures and diagrams, with fewer words, reducing the issues associated with providing multiple language translations. Again, make it easy for the customer to use our product.

6. Prime the Distribution Channel: If our company sells through Distribution as well as Direct, then there is the additional intermediary to consider. The Distributors will also need the "how to" guides on ordering, managing, and using the products. In fact, the Distributor will need everything an end customer will need. Further, if the new product replaces an old product or previous version, we should prepare for conversations about disposition of the existing inventory. Will we take it back? Are we providing incentives to sell it? The approach we take has cost implications, but also impacts the speed of channel conversion. We must create a plan for managing the Distribution channel.

Formulate the IP Strategy

At a high level, the topic of Intellectual Property seems pretty simple: we want to file whatever we can, as soon as we can. IP forms one of the best barriers to competitors, so an extensive, comprehensive IP portfolio can help maximize our period of exclusivity in the market. That is, the feature or benefit that sets us apart from the Next Best Alternative may be something we can patent. By doing so, we create a significant barrier to entry for competitors who would otherwise take market share and drive down price with similar "me too" products. Filing and protecting our IP can be critical to maximizing the Growth phase. However, there are some details to keep in mind.

First, the IP strategy must be decided and filings created *before* the product is launched. As part of the ongoing VOC process to create and refine the Value Prop, we will want to consider showing prototypes or samples to customers. Our IP filings need to be in place before we show our ideas to the customer, even if we are working under a Non-disclosure Agreement (NDA).

Second, we should consider that creating a proprietary solution may impact the speed of customer adoption. How important is this to us? By being different, our product has a strong Value Prop, but it now has this hurdle to overcome in order to gain traction. Is our Value Prop so compelling that we can obtain exclusivity, which is clearly our preference? Or, must we consider licensing the invention to another supplier? The time to think about this is before we launch the product.

Finally, we have to evaluate the impact of IP and new technology on the ecosystem. In our earlier assessment, did we find other products or tools which will need access to our IP in order to ensure compatibility? We might need to license a supplier of a complementary product in order to facilitate the development of the ecosystem.

Create the Pricing Strategy

From our Value Prop, we should have an excellent idea of the quantifiable benefit our product delivers to the customer, which in turn informs us of the price premium we can reasonably achieve. With that information, we can decide on our approach to pricing. We basically have two options: price at a premium, or price for rapid adoption.

1. Price premium: We would prefer to price the product at the full premium that is supported by the Value Prop. Price premiums are hard to get, and they don't last forever, so we want to take this approach if we are confident the customer will acknowledge the value the product delivers. This is one of the main reasons our Value Prop must be quantified, and whenever possible, dollarized. We expect competition. New alternatives will eventually be introduced, and price pressure is sure to materialize sooner or later. But, because every dollar of price concession flows straight to the bottom line of the P&L, we want to preserve the premium for as long as possible.

   However, we should remember that a price premium can also delay customer adoption, especially if the customer has a bureaucratic product approval network. For example, imagine that the entire benefit of the product is for the customer's Engineering department, but also imagine that Procurement has a voice in the approval process. Engineering may be excited to approve the product, but Procurement will not be anxious to pay more. Or, imagine that the Value Prop is simply not intuitive to all parties involved in the approval process. The Value Prop may need to be presented over and over again to multiple layers in the customer's organizational structure, where it is likely to be met with varying degrees of skepticism. As you may recall from our earlier discussion on various product lifecycle curves, the more intuitive the Value Prop, the more rapid the adoption, and delayed adoption means delayed Revenue. This is one reason we anticipate the customer approval process as part of pre-Launch planning. Also, once we show the product to the customer, we should assume the competitors become aware of it, if they weren't already. If we want to realize the price premium, we must be extremely confident in the strength of our Value Prop, and in our barriers to entry.

2. Price for rapid adoption: Alternatively, we might take the approach to trade some or all of the theoretical price premium for increased share or more rapid conversion of the market. We might trade price for preference. This makes sense in a few scenarios:

- The market is torn between two competing technologies, and we want to establish our version as the standard. In a highly fragmented market, early widespread adoption can be the key to long-term sustainability.
- The barriers to entry are not strong or are not sustainable, so gaining market share actually has more long-term benefit than a short-lived price premium.
- The product can be leveraged to win or strengthen a position at a strategic customer, possibly in support of other product lines, future products, or to capture anticipated future growth.
- Product sales may be needed in the short term to achieve our higher level corporate financial goals.

Anticipate the Competitive Response

To further complicate matters, our Launch planning MUST consider some contingencies! At some point, the Bad Guys will figure out what we are doing. In the best case, this will happen when we launch our product. More likely, they may hear things from our target customers. If they aggressively comb IP filings, they may put the puzzle together before the Launch. Or, they may already be aware of the unmet customer need, and are working on their own solution. Regardless, we should anticipate a competitive response and prepare for it. If the roles were reversed, and they introduced the new product, what would we do?

At a minimum, we should prepare for two responses.

1. FUD: The competitors will likely launch a campaign of Fear, Uncertainty and Doubt. They will tell the market and customers that our product has reliability or safety concerns; that the customer is taking a risk even using it; that it doesn't really solve the

fundamental problem or alleviate the unmet need; that any price premium is unjustified; that we will be unable to supply, etc. Upon hearing the FUD campaign, the customer may start to worry they have missed something or made a mistake. They may want more testing, or additional time to reconsider the impact of the change. They may want a safer alternative. Depending on how convinced the customer is by the FUD, our Value Prop may have been weakened. The separation between our product and the Next Best Alternative may have been eroded. Or, even if the customer does not believe the FUD arguments, they may still leverage those same arguments against us to get better terms or a lower price in a negotiation.

How should we respond? First, we need to understand the magnitude of the threat. How convincing is the FUD campaign, and is the customer buying into it? Are there legitimate concerns we failed to consider, or is this simply "Marketing spin"? It may be tempting to reduce the price in the face of a FUD campaign to "close the deal" and move on, but this should never be our first response! Protecting price as much as possible is critical to achieving our Business Case assumptions, and to the long-term viability of the product. We will probably never recover any price we give up, and we should not lose confidence in our Value Prop in the face of an unfounded FUD campaign. Instead, we should combat the FUD campaign by reiterating the Value Prop, reiterating our thorough testing, and offering increased support. Test data can often take the emotion out of a discussion, and is particularly effective when confronted with fear, uncertainty and doubt. Test data is something we should have in abundance, while the competitor only has theories. We have built and tested the product; they have only heard about it. If there is real concern the customer will delay adoption, we might consider alternatives to price, such as increasing the warranty period, promising dedicated field support, committing capacity, or other *targeted* measures that address the specific customer concerns. While these have cost implications, they are almost always preferable to a price reduction.

2. Price Pressure: We should also be prepared for a price reduction on the current Next Best Alternative. Once again, this ties back to the criticality of creating an accurate Value Prop. By truly

understanding and quantifying the cost of the customer problem or unmet need, we were able to develop a pricing strategy and justify a price premium. However, if the competitor lowers the price of the Next Best Alternative, our price premium baseline has changed, and our Value Prop has been weakened.

A price reduction by the incumbent is a bit different than a FUD campaign. We almost certainly will have to offer some kind of concession, and we should plan for this as part of the Pricing Strategy. However, we should always remember there are alternatives to price, and we need not abandon our strategy as a knee-jerk reaction to the competitor. As with the FUD response, an extended warranty, a capacity commitment, field support, or other measures may be valued enough by the customer to offset the competitive price pressure.

However, despite our best efforts, there is a good chance a price drop by the incumbent supplier will require a price decrease from us, so we need to be prepared in advance for that contingency. Let's assume our preference, as determined during pre-Launch planning, is to introduce the product at the full price premium based on the Value Prop. If the competitor responds by lowering price on their incumbent product, then we may consider shifting to a market penetration strategy. That is, we will provide our product at a lower premium, maybe even at price-parity, in exchange for an increased share, a longer supply commitment, an exclusivity period, or something else which is high value to us, and low cost to the customer. Alternatively, we may even know in advance that what we really want is quick adoption. We might want to land an anchor customer to get traction in the market and begin to generate economies of scale in purchasing and manufacturing. In that case, expecting there will probably be a price response from the competitor, we may still *lead* with a price premium, and then *settle* for the product preference we really wanted in the first place.

There are many, many possible scenarios, but two general rules apply:

- Our initial response to a competitive threat should not immediately be to lower price! Always look for alternatives.
- If we do lower price, we should ALWAYS ask for something in return, such as exclusivity, increased volume, or extended contract duration.

Prepare for Customer Support

A "new" product is not just new to the market, it is new to our internal organization as well. Our internal support groups must be prepared for the product Launch, and this begins with the frontline of customer interaction, the Customer Service team. Just as customers need information about the product – what it is, how to use it, why to buy it – our internal Customer Service team needs to be prepared for the Launch and for subsequent support. Customer Service is typically the primary touch point with the customer, and must have the information and tools to make it easy to support customers who buy and use the product. Prior to Launch, Product Managers should ensure the Customer Service team has:

- Context: What the product is, what problem it solves, why customers should want it.
- Access to Detailed Information: How to find answers to unforeseen technical questions. Who are the experts?
- Supporting Documentation: Product information sheets, Marketing collateral, installation, operation, storage and handling procedures, and other supporting documentation.
- Order Entry Capability: Systems necessary to take an order for any of the product variations we have decided to offer.

Just as we endeavor to make it easy for the customer to *use* the product, we also must endeavor to make it easy for the customer to *buy* the product.

Prepare for Field Support

Service after the sale is important as well. We will certainly have instances where a user has problems with the product. It could be they don't have all the necessary training or documentation, or they might be using the product in an application we had not considered, or they may even have a defective product that escaped our quality controls. Regardless the cause, we should prepare for customer support after the sale. This service typically must be somewhat technical, and should be prepared to deal with frustrated users. What is our plan for field support? Do we have a dedicated team? Will support be during normal business hours, or 24x7? How will customers reach the support team? Will it be electronically, via our website? Will we provide a dedicated phone number to call? Or do we always want Customer Service to be the first point of contact? What additional tools and information does the Field Support team need, above and beyond what is needed by Customer Service?

Ready the Internal Systems

Our supply chain and internal Manufacturing Systems must also be prepared to plan, schedule, produce, and ship a new product. Most large companies rely on an Enterprise Resource Planning (ERP) system for major portions of the supply chain. ERP systems are essential once operations reach a certain size in order to integrate the complexities of planning, operations, and reporting. These systems provide tremendous benefits, but they also require the user to input the correct information and "rules" in order to be useful.

- Do we have the new product part numbers established in our ERP system? Have we defined which product variations and customizations are acceptable, and which are not? Does this match what was provided to Customer Service and Field Support?
- If the product utilizes new materials or new suppliers, do we have them correctly set up in our ERP system? Are we dealing with "approved" suppliers? Are Raw Material Specifications in place? Are there new QA material checks required? Do we have any "Make v. Buy" decisions to make on materials and sub-assemblies?
- Are the Manufacturing Instructions established, such as Bills of Materials, Work Centers, and Product Routings to allow the product to flow through the factory?
- Have we established an appropriate quality plan to minimize unnecessary costs and delays? This might include increased in-process or final inspections until enough information is available to support a more effective "build-in" approach to quality.
- Do we have capabilities in place to allow financial reporting, inventory tracking, scrap measurement, and other necessary performance measurements?

Create an Integrated Supply and Demand Forecast

Returning to our earlier discussion, a successful Launch begins with a great plan. No plan is truly great unless it is documented, communicated, and thoroughly understood. We all must be on the same page, and that is especially true when it comes to aligning capacity with demand.

Launch incorporates many intrinsic and extrinsic factors, some of which *influence* the rollout plan, and some of which place *rigid constraints* on what we can actually do. In many instances, the capacity plan falls into the latter category. During Launch we have a simple rule: **Ensure product availability. Don't run out of capacity!** Imagine the scenario where we have done everything right. We have correctly addressed an unmet customer need. We have a product that carries a price premium because it solves the customer's problem. We are primed for a period of exclusivity as our product and Value Prop quickly gain traction. We launch the product...and cannot deliver. Short of a fatal quality problem, not many scenarios would be more painful and frustrating for the customers, the company...and the Product Manager. We can literally kill our new product if we cannot deliver.

However, we cannot have infinite capacity. Capacity comes with a cost and a lead time. Some businesses are extremely capital-intensive, and the introduction of a new product is inherently risky because it requires investment before there are sales. We may find ourselves in a bit of a conundrum: without sales, it is difficult to justify the investment for capacity, but without the capacity, we cannot achieve the sales. Ultimately, this is resolved through confidence in the Business Case assumptions, which tie directly back to how well we have assessed the Root Want in developing a solution. Still, we will need an iterative process to create and communicate a plan which clearly demonstrates how the capacity and demand are aligned. What this means, then, is we must work through multiple iterations of the demand forecast and the capacity forecast, continually asking the reciprocal questions:

How will we have *capacity* to fill the customer *demand?*

How will we have customer *demand* to fill the available *capacity?*

The following is a generic process to follow to work through these iterations:

1. Create an Unconstrained Demand Forecast

   Ideally, we would prefer to put capacity in place that allows for maximum sales. We launch products for commercial reasons, to realize profitable sales from the market. Our preference is to capture ALL the available demand. And so, we begin the process by creating a demand forecast that is not constrained by capacity.

This is not to say the unconstrained demand forecast ignores real, known *market* constraints. It simply means we use our knowledge of the market and customers to assess the total opportunity. Put another way, the deliverable is simply this: **All things considered,** what is our best estimate of the commercial demand we could achieve if we have no internal limitations? How much demand is there?

These items should have already been considered in developing the Business Case, but probably need updating.

- What is the total size of the addressable market?
- How mature is the ecosystem? Does it vary among customers or market segments? How will it impact the product adoption rate?
- Are we dealing with a few large, key customers, or is the market fragmented? What is the size (potential demand) from each element or segment of the market?
- What is the channel strategy? Do we sell direct, through distribution, to OEMs, or some combination?
- How are we segmenting the Launch? Are we launching the product with a splash, or are we taking a more surgical approach, going after one customer at a time? Is our customer base homogenous, or do we have a mix of customer types and channel strategies?
- What did we learn when we assessed the customer approval processes, and how does this affect the timing and magnitude in the demand forecast?
- What are the optimistic, pessimistic, and most likely product adoption scenarios?
- Did we price for quick adoption or for a premium? How will this affect the demand forecast?

2. Create the Capacity Forecast

   Now, understanding the commercial opportunity, *what would it take* from a capacity perspective to deliver the unconstrained demand? What would it cost, and *is it worth it?*

   Capacity can be constrained in a number of different ways, and limitations in any area can determine the overall capacity. It is important to consider what we have, what we can achieve, and the cost and timing to get there.

Equipment: What equipment will be used to manufacture the new product? Are we buying new equipment, renovating existing equipment, or are we able to simply use the existing equipment as-is? If new or renovated equipment is to be used, what is the lead time needed to make it available? Is it days, weeks or months? The longer the lead time, the more complicated the evaluation. What is the cost? The more expensive the equipment and modifications, the greater the risk of being wrong on the demand forecast. If we are using existing equipment, is there available capacity, or is the equipment already fully utilized?

People: How many trained operators do we need? How long does it take to train them? During Launch, the manufacturing process may be more art than science, so we may be constrained by a limited supply of trained operators. We may even be relying on expert Technicians under the supervision of the Technology or Engineering teams to manufacture the initial products. Before we Launch, we need a plan for how we will ensure a sufficient quantity of trained operators.

Materials: Does our new product use existing materials, from existing suppliers, with a well-established supply chain? Or, are we introducing a new element of uncertainty with new suppliers or new materials? Have we provided our material suppliers with a demand forecast, and have they provided a capacity commitment? Consider the risks this can create, and ensure there is a clear path to sufficient material availability.

Method: Are manufacturing procedures established for the new product to support the machine and people? Are new or revised work instructions required? Are new Work Centers needed? Are the Manufacturing systems able to track inventory, receipt materials, process transactions, and conduct financial reporting?

3. Apply Reality Filters and Iterate for the Best Solution
   Now, understanding both the unconstrained demand and the cost and timing of capacity, we can make intelligent business decisions about the best course of action. There is no "one size fits all"

approach to harmonizing the supply and demand plans, since each Launch has its own unique risks and rewards, and each capacity plan has its own costs and limitations. We must also consider our level of confidence in our assumptions, our ability to adjust either the capacity or the demand plan, and possible contingencies for unforeseen events. We must consider not only the cost of the plan, but also the *cost of being wrong*. Some additional considerations as we make these business decisions include:

- What is our confidence in the timing of the Technology plan? Are we confident in the product availability dates? Both the Manufacturing and Commercial plans depend on these!
- How does the market/customer segmentation allow us to adjust the product Launch plan if we must accommodate hard limits on capacity?
- What is our confidence in the speed of customer adoption? What is the risk the unconstrained demand forecast will come slower than expected? Could it be faster?
- What is our confidence in the volume of the customer adoption? What is the risk the demand will come lower than the forecast? What are the chances it will be higher?
- How much risk is associated with adding capacity? Are we confident in the production yields? Is capacity simply a matter of adding machines and operators, or are we dealing with some art amid the science?
- What is the cost of accelerating the capacity plan?
- How nimble is the capacity plan? Can it be easily adjusted if the commercial adoption goes better or worse than expected?
- What incremental triggers and trip points can we set to mitigate risk as the Launch results unfold? For example, we may agree internally that we will act to add additional capacity once we have converted an anchor customer.

4. Document, Communicate, Track and Revise the Plan
   Because Launch is an event that stretches across the organization, clearly communicating the plan is vital to facilitating successful execution. The Technology, Manufacturing and Commercial elements of Launch are mutually dependent on one another, and the highlights of each should be captured **in a single picture**. This

facilitates broader understanding and enables the impact of an unforeseen event to be more readily understood by all players, especially Leadership, to drive the plan to successful completion. This view of the plan should include:

- Product availability dates from the Technology plan: This does not mean every item or milestone from the product development plan, but only those that directly reflect changes in product availability. When will we have a working prototype or a product for a field trial? When can we provide some limited capacity under Technology supervision? If we expect customers to require certification data, such as from a 3rd party, when do we expect that to be available?
- Customer conversion dates from the Commercial plan: When will we approach customers? What does their qualification and acceptance timing look like?
- Demand Forecast: Based on our plans for releasing the product, what demand do we anticipate?
- Capacity Forecast: What is the capacity plan to support the demand forecast? When does equipment become available? Will we adjust the Commercial Plan or the Manufacturing Plan in the event of a mismatch?
  - o If the plan shows a capacity shortfall v. demand, how will we cover it?
  - o If the plan shows excess capacity, how will we use it? Will we build stock, hold it as headroom for unforeseen events, or try to find incremental demand to consume it?

Capturing these key elements on a single page allows the interrelations and dependencies to be more readily understood, and the implications of an unforeseen event are more apparent. Since the Product Manager is relying on leadership and influence to accomplish key elements of the Launch, this view is critical to create organizational buy-in, ensuring that we are literally all on the same page.

A simple, generic example is shown in Figure 6.1.

Figure 6.1 Integrated View of Supply, Demand, Tech Milestones

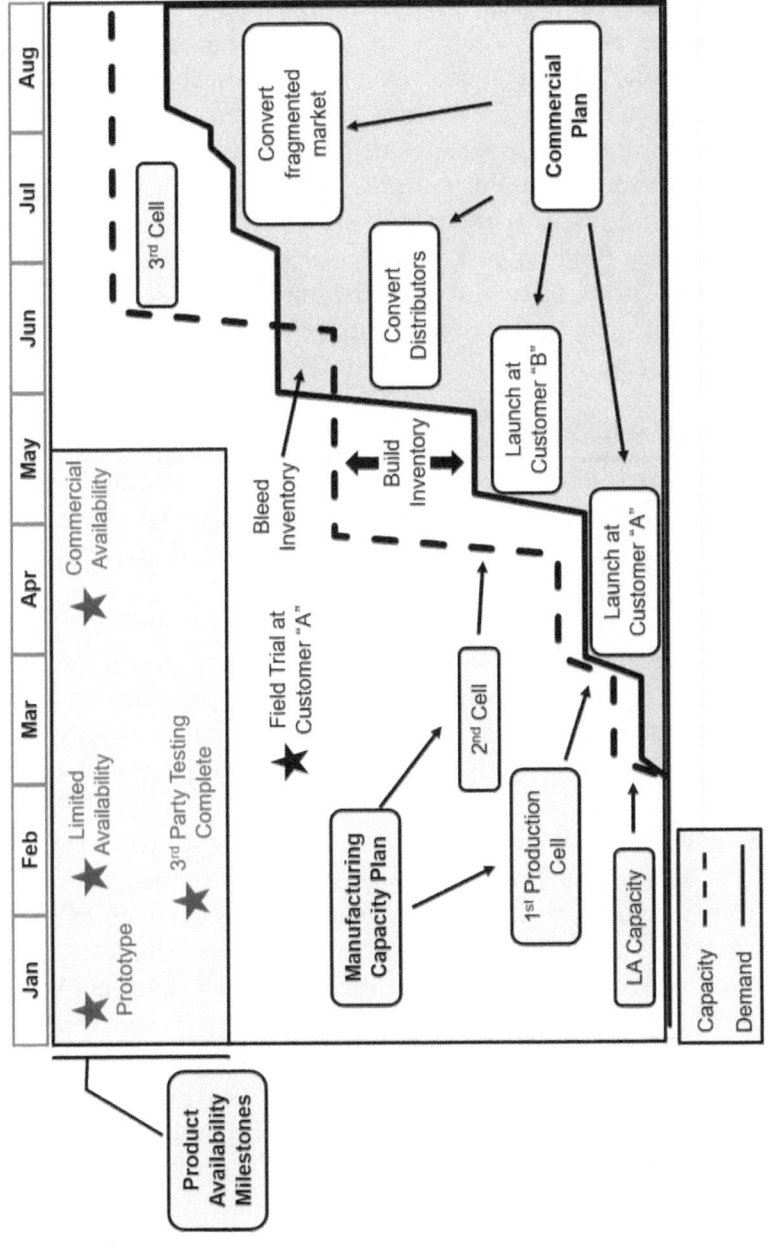

Create the Scorecard

Finally, before we Launch, we have to know what success looks like. We have a plan, and as we start to get results, we want to understand and communicate how we are tracking v. that plan. We also want to determine what adjustments are necessary to improve. The scorecard should directly reflect the most critical items from the Business Case and from the Launch plan. As mentioned earlier, we should be careful that what we include in the scorecard does not cause us to make a wrong turn. For example, assume our plan is to achieve a price premium, even at the expense of speed of adoption. If we include a metric for first year product sales, we might create undue pressure to lower price to hit the metric. A scorecard is a communication and tracking tool, but it also drives behavior. What gets measured gets done!

Post-Launch Execution

Once we have done a thorough job of pre-Launch planning, the post-Launch goal is to identify and **react with urgency** to items that are not going according to plan, or things we missed in the planning process. This is what is meant by violent execution. There are tools which allow us to identify the most likely and impactful risks and issues, and we should utilize these in the planning process and add contingencies to the plan. However, we could never know in advance exactly *which* issues we will experience. I am reminded of the story of the boss who asked for a list of all the unforeseen problems they would encounter!

The key, then, is to maintain organizational alignment and awareness on the execution of the plan. This requires dedicated effort and frequent update, with a team focused on post-Launch execution to the exclusion of anything else. Some items can be a nuisance, others can literally destroy the product. Specifically, some areas to emphasize:

1. Improve Quality and Field Performance: The product will not survive into Growth unless we immediately and thoroughly address any field issues. Are defects being reported? What is the return rate on the product? What are the causes for these returns? Any quality problems must be dealt with quickly and thoroughly. Rapid correction is critical!
2. Validate the Value Prop: As soon as possible, we need confirmation from the customer that the product is addressing the unmet need.

If not, what is wrong? What are we missing? How can we correct? For items that are not integral to the Business Case, we should begin collecting VOC for future iterations of product attributes and features to improve the user experience.

3. Assess Customer Adoption: Are the target customers responding as we expected? Have they asked for additional information, documentation, or samples? What, if anything, is delaying customer acceptance of the product? Are they buying the quantities we anticipated? How can we address any problems?

4. Evaluate the Competitive Response: How are the competitors responding? Have they launched a FUD campaign, challenged our IP, or changed the price on the incumbent product? What is our response? Is it effective? What other options do we have?

5. Resolve Organizational Readiness: We almost certainly had some gaps in our planning and preparation. Was our internal training of the support groups satisfactory? Did we reach everyone? What gaps do we need to resolve?

6. Correct the Product Collateral: What did we miss? Did we create a book where we should have made a video? Did we release documentation in the right languages? Are there outdated instructions and procedures in the marketplace that we need to somehow eliminate and replace?

7. Validate Technology: Did we miss any requirements or expectations in the development process? For example, is the product used in an environment or application we did not anticipate? Is more testing required? Going back to the quality and field issues, is the product suitable for the laboratory environment, but not the "real world"?

8. Evaluate Manufacturing: Are we getting the costs, productivity, and quality output we expected? It is reasonable to expect these metrics to be unfavorable compared to Mature, legacy products. Costs will be higher due to manufacturing inefficiencies, such as lack of scale, lack of manufacturing experience, supply chain inefficiencies, and perhaps the need for specialty materials, but are they what one would expect for a new product? Are lines coming into production as planned? Is the operator training going as expected?

9. Finally, all things considered, are we **on track** to deliver the Business Case? Because the capacity and demand forecasts are so related to each other, we need to continually update the integrated

plan based on the success of the Launch.

We will almost certainly find multiple issues to correct. Identifying these issues is one thing; prioritizing and correcting them is another. The Launch team must determine the business criticality of each issue and prioritize the corrective actions. A general guide for prioritization:

1. Primary attention should be given to those issues which threaten the viability of the product, such as field quality issues.
2. Next, to those which threaten the Business Case assumptions, such as customer adoption rate and availability of supply.
3. Then, to those which sub-optimize the Launch, such as training and collateral.
4. Finally, to opportunities for improvement, such as additional features or attributes to accentuate the Value Prop.

As we have seen, planning and execution go hand-in-hand in the Launch phase. Thorough planning, followed by violent execution, will lead us into the best phase in the lifecycle: Growth.

Figure 6.2   Launch Checklist

Assess the Ecosystem	Ensure seamless integration of the product with the environment
Ancillary and Interfacing products	Verify availability and operation; identify and address gaps
Tools and Methods	Modify as required
Legal and Regulatory	Verify product compliance
Industry Standards and Protocols	Ensure compliance of product and features

Cultivate the Commercial Environment	Prepare for Customer interaction
Customer Positioning Statements	Compelling, focused statements from Value Prop; target by customer persona
Product Promotional Plan	Where, how, when to Launch; Plan to raise awareness, generate excitement
Anticipate Customer Approval Process	Whose approval required? Timing? Samples? Trials? Testing/Certification?
Customer Training Plan	How to order, use, store, handle the product
Product Collateral	Create or update catalogs, spec sheets, advertisements, product samples

Formulate the IP Strategy	Protect and leverage IP to the best advantage
File IP	Act on IP opportunities to ensure protection and barriers to entry
Establish NDAs	Protect IP before engaging customers
IP Licensing	Consider opportunity/need to enhance ecosystem and drive adoption

Figure 6.2 Launch Checklist, continued

Create the Pricing Strategy	Determine best use of the product advantages
Calculate Price Premium from Value Prop	Quantify and dollarize Value Prop
Decide on approach to market	Price Premium v. Speed of Adoption and standardization
Consider contingencies	Anticipate customer pricing pushback

Anticipate the Competitive Response	Prepare for competitive headwinds
Fear, Uncertainty, Doubt (FUD)	Reiterate VP; prepare data; consider alternatives to price concessions
Price Pressure	Reiterate VP; prepare data; consider alternatives to price concessions

Train the Customer Support Team	Ensure organizational readiness
Context	What the product is, what problem it solves, why customers should want it
Access to detailed information	Where to find answers to technical questions; Who are the experts?
Documentation and collateral	Access to all collateral: installation, operation, storage, handling
Order entry capability	Systems ready to take an order for any approved product variation

Prepare for Field Support	Facilitate product usage
Determine support model	24x7 or other? Define the team and provide training, tools
Access field support	Customer access: phone, website, via Customer Service, other?

Figure 6.2   Launch Checklist, continued

Ready the Internal Systems	Ensure system and production capabilities
ERP and Manufacturing Systems	Load part numbers, create Work Centers, BOMs and Routings
Define allowable product variations	Create product boundaries
Suppliers and Materials	Qualify new suppliers and new materials; verify capacity
Manufacturing capability	Manufacturing instructions, reporting and tracking, operator training
Quality plan to support production	Sampling and inspection plan created

Integrated Supply v. Demand Forecast	Facilitate internal planning, communication, consensus, adjustment
Unconstrained demand forecast	Considering all market forces, best estimate of commercial demand v. time assuming no capacity constraints
Capacity plan	Assess cost to match capacity with unconstrained demand; Consider equipment, people, methods, materials
Reconcile Supply v. Demand	Cost v. benefit decisions of matching capacity to demand. Include risks, uncertainties, potential contingencies
Document and communicate plan	Create integrated plan for product availability, capacity, demand

Create the scorecard	Track success v. Business Case assumptions and plan
Choose appropriate metrics	Ensure metrics match the plan and drive right behavior
Review frequently and update plan	Aggressively react to performance v. plan; adjust actions as needed

Compendium

- Product Launch is about thorough planning and violent execution. Plan your work, and work your plan!
- Anticipate a competitive response that includes FUD and price reduction on the Next Best Alternative.
- Assess and facilitate development of the ecosystem to support seamless adoption of the product.
- Prepare for customer interaction with focused product positioning statements, collateral and training.
- Anticipate the customer approval process to avoid unnecessary delays to adoption.
- Establish Intellectual Property as a critical barrier to competitive entry throughout the product lifecycle.
- Develop a pricing strategy based on the Value Prop. A price premium is preferred; in some cases, consider trading price for volume, share, or rapid adoption.
- Establish organizational readiness: thoroughly train Customer Service and establish the field support structure.
- Prepare the internal systems to support manufacture and sale of the product.
- Aggressively monitor field feedback; act quickly on quality, performance, and logistics issues.
- Keep capacity ahead of demand; Add quality checks to prevent problems from reaching the customer.
- Track sales and product performance v. the Business Case; make course adjustments as necessary.
- Validate the Value Prop and look for opportunities to improve.

Chapter 7
GROWTH

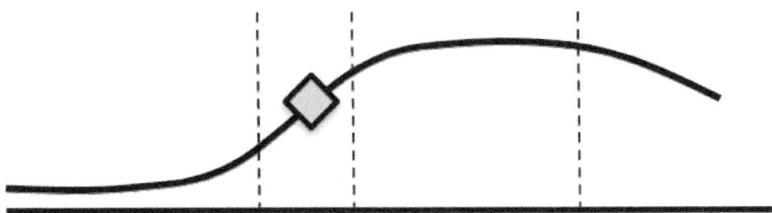

"If you have everything under control, you're not moving fast enough."
Mario Andretti

Having successfully Launched our product, our Value Prop becomes increasingly understood as we steam into the Growth phase. The Growth phase is the time when sales increase disproportionately to our investments of time and money. Pre-Launch planning is an exercise of faith: we invest considerable time and effort for a product with no sales. Launch is an exciting and tense time as we adapt urgently to new information, seeking validation of our Value Prop in the form of market adoption. Growth is when the Value Prop hits a tipping point. Customers *get it*. Market pull for the product emerges. This is the best time of a product's life. This is when we see the Business Case begin to be realized. Growth is "show me the money" time. Everyone wants to be part of the Growth phase.

Including the competitors.

The competitive response will almost certainly include an alternative product, a lower price, or both, and will erode our Value Prop by changing the Next Best Alternative, and ushering in high price pressure. The clock on the golden age is ticking. Growth is full speed ahead while we fight off emerging threats that would drag the product prematurely into the Mature phase. Our goal is to maximize sales, but what does that mean for the Product Manager? Where do we focus now?

Grow the Demand

We call this the Growth phase for a reason. As the market comes to understand our solution and our Value Prop, further promotion leads to disproportionate returns. Now is the time to put the accelerator to the floor and get the most out of the market!

Maximize Sales from Existing Customers

Our Value Prop resonates with our initial target customers. How can we sell them more? Can we get more share? Can we accelerate their conversion? What is holding them back from 100% adoption? Do they have other operations, offices, branches or locations that could also generate demand? Since they already see the value of the product, they can potentially create additional pull for it. We can't possibly have full knowledge of the inner workings of all our customers, but we can partner with them to identify other possible opportunities for our product. **Selling more to existing customers is the most efficient way to grow the product.**

Expand the Customer Base

Are there other customers who have the same Root Want as our existing customers, such as those within the same demographic? This might include competitors to our original target customers. A "copy / paste" rollout to these is an efficient and effective way to grow sales.

Another opportunity is to evaluate adjacent customers, markets and regions. Unfortunately, although these can represent big opportunities for growth, we may not have the necessary access to address them easily. We may not have commercial contacts at these customers, or our supply chain may not be capable of reaching them, or product modifications might be required for the specific market. At a minimum, we should understand these opportunities, and the barriers that we would have to overcome. What would it take to gain traction in these areas?

Rebranding may be another possibility. Is our "consumer" product suitable for "industrial" applications? We may be able to sell the same product under a different name or different part number to a different market, expanding our commercial base without additional product development. These opportunities typically require some significant investigation, so this may be more appropriate for the Mature phase, but it is never too early to identify additional sales opportunities.

Promote, Promote, Promote

The key to expanding sales in all cases is to evangelize the Value Prop. We know we have a good message; what we need is for more potential customers to hear it. Targeted advertising is essential in this regard, and the promotional medium depends on the product and the market. The avenue to reach customers in the consumer market is obviously different than for B2B products.

It's a classic Marketing problem: what is the best avenue to raise customer awareness for our product? Especially for B2B products, we should publish articles in appropriate journals and offer papers and presentations at various trade shows, chronicling our successes. Whenever possible, these should include testimonials and specific customer success stories. We may ask a customer to co-author an article, chronicling their experience.

Expand the Channel Strategy

As we grow, we will likely find ourselves needing more paths in order to reach more customers. This is especially true if our growth is in a fragmented market, where we could benefit from some consolidation of the demand, or if we have decided to pursue market or regional adjacencies, perhaps in places where we do not currently have a strong presence. As customers "pull" for our solution, we need the means to connect their demand with our supply, which often means Distributors. The Distributor becomes an extension of our Sales force by reaching the wider audience. They may carry inventory to mitigate demand spikes and enable shorter lead time. The right Distributor can help drive the ecosystem by providing the ancillary products that "go with" our solution. Securing Distributors will also help entrench our product as the market standard, and will be an effective barrier to competitors. Finally, we will almost certainly need Distributors for the later product lifecycles. Of course, all of this comes at a financial cost, but maximizing sales during the Growth phase will almost certainly make it worthwhile.

Depending on the product, other channels to consider might

include OEMs, who incorporate our product into their product. This might even include co-branding (e.g., "Intel Inside"). Additionally, we can seek out contractors, installers, service groups, and "authorized dealers" who can help drive standardization of our solution.

Improve the Competitive Position

We might compare the Growth phase to the perfect vacation spot. Whether you like the beach, the mountains, amusement parks, or international cities, one thing is certain: a huge crowd can ruin the experience. Competitors who enter the game during the Growth phase are like that crowd. They bring competitive offerings that can take away share while at the same time driving down prices. The Growth phase is attractive because of *exclusivity*. Competition ushers in the Mature phase as it pushes the market toward commoditization. We must urgently respond to the competitive threats to protect the benefits of the Growth phase!

Address the Competitive Response and Fortify Barriers to Entry

During the Launch section we discussed FUD and price pressure as probable immediate competitive responses. As we said then, our goal is to counteract these responses by reiterating our Value Prop, providing additional data, and offering valued services as alternatives to lowering price. Now the competition has had time to study the problem and to see and understand our solution. We should expect more than just an ongoing FUD campaign; we must prepare for competing product solutions. Those solutions are likely to come in one of two ways.

1. The Competitive "Knock-off"

In this case, the competitors may introduce a copy of our product. Consider the plethora of generic over-the-counter drugs that compete with name brands. These products are typically marketed as 1-for-1 substitutes for the name brand. The dosage and active ingredients are usually the same. They are typically stocked next to the original product on store shelves, and often have similar packaging to the original. In many cases, they will even invite comparison to the name brand. E.g., "Compare to the active ingredient in..."

How do we protect against these? For most products, the greatest barrier to generics is Intellectual Property. This is, again, why we placed such emphasis on determining the IP strategy prior to Launch. IP filings are critical to keeping generic "knock offs" out of the market during the Growth phase.

Technology may also form an effective barrier. If our product requires an invention, then this certainly can delay or dissuade competitors from entering the market. If the product requires an invention that is also IP protected, then we have a solid barrier.

Another barrier to generic competitors is through the use of branding. DuPont, for example, has been extremely effective at entrenching its brand names onto product solutions. Kevlar®, Nomex®, Tyvek®, Styrofoam™, and Sorona® are just a few examples of registered brands from DuPont. DuPont has been so effective in this practice that many people may only know the DuPont brand name, and not the generic equivalent. Once a brand name becomes part of the vernacular, even making its way into customer specifications, it is difficult to displace.

Finally, our solution may be rooted in another core competency, such as precision manufacturing, our extensive supply chain, or something else. Similar to Technology, these competencies can provide competitive advantages that will be difficult to overcome.

Make no mistake, the competitors will end our exclusivity if given a chance. Thorough and effective barriers to entry are critical!

2. The Competing Solution

While these barriers may keep competitors from *copying* our product, they will not prevent them from offering their own solution to the customer's problem. Our product Launch not only highlights the customer's Root Want, it also draws attention to the money that can be made by addressing it. Despite IP and other barriers that preclude competitors from copying our solution, they may still develop a different product of their own. Again, competition will spoil our exclusivity, reduce our share, drive down price, and ultimately hasten our solution into commoditization and Maturity. What's more, the competitive offering may rely on a different, competing ecosystem, meaning there may only be room for one solution. There may only be one survivor.

Cultivate the Ecosystem

We cannot forget about the ecosystem, even after a successful Launch. Our product still must function with other products, procedures, protocols and accessories. In Growth, it gets a little easier to drive those ecosystem items that were previously out of our control. Consider the example of the compact disc. CD players did not become commonplace in cars until the Value Prop of the CD was well understood and accepted. Then, the CD advantage drove automakers to make changes. Or, as with the Microsoft Zune example, the incumbent Apple music players solidified their foothold as a result of a five-year head start, with the ecosystem becoming populated with compatible accessories. An ecosystem came to be built around the iPod family, further entrenching it as the market leader.

As a more striking example, consider the linkage between the ecosystem and the competitive landscape as it pertained to home video recordings during the 1970s and 80s, when JVC's VHS® and Sony's Betamax® technologies competed for the market. Sony launched the Betamax in 1975 as one of the first affordable, commercially available home video solutions. A year later, JVC introduced the competing VHS format. Importantly, the recording technologies were built around different form factors. Betamax cassettes did not fit in VHS machines, and vice versa. Since consumers would not buy two different systems for the same Root Want, the market would inevitably standardize on one solution. The better Value Prop would win.

Betamax not only had the first-mover advantage, it was arguably the superior technology. Betamax offered better picture quality, slightly better sound quality, and better image stabilization. However, the original Betamax could only record for up to 60 minutes on a single tape. VHS had a maximum standard recording time of 120 minutes, making it more compatible with standard-length movies. And, the VHS recorders were lower cost. In an era of CRT televisions, before the advent of improved resolution that would come with plasma and LED technologies, the video quality advantages of Betamax were not valued by the market as much as the longer recording time and lower cost of the VHS format. The VHS ecosystem flourished, and the Betamax ecosystem began to collapse. Despite being first to market, with a theoretically superior product, Sony lost because of a lack of understanding of what was valued most by the market. This example highlights the interrelation of the ecosystem and the competitive landscape. Competitive offerings can do more than take share and drive down price; they can usher in the end for our solution. Sometimes the market will only support one ecosystem.

This also takes us back to the product creation process. There is no substitute for clear understanding of the customer's problems and Root Wants. This is why we continually assess the Value Prop in terms of the Root Want, and why we continue to evaluate the Next Best Alternative, which can change at any time. We can use competitive intelligence to help us figure out how the competitors plan to compete. Follow the IP filings, press releases and industry papers from our competitors to see where they are headed.

Enhance the Value Prop with Features and Attributes

We launched the product based on our understanding of the customer's problem. Although we exercised considerable effort in identifying the Root Want, our understanding is almost certainly imperfect. Now, with the product gaining momentum in the market, we have a critical opportunity to fine tune and improve the Value Prop. What are the users saying about the product? How can we make it better? "It's great, except for…" Or, "It would be even better if…"

Most important is to consider feedback that directly relates to the Root Want, but we should also look for ways to improve the entire user experience, such as ease of use, ergonomics, colors, materials, and features. For example, should we add a built-in level to a cabinet that mounts on a wall, or install a better grip on a new tool or device, or work to improve the battery life on an electrical product? These may not directly relate to the Root Want, but we have a golden opportunity to improve the user experience and enhance our position.

Robert Wang is the inventor of the Instant Pot®, a multi-use cooker that is in the Growth phase as of this writing. The Instant Pot has tens of thousands of reviews on Amazon, but Wang says, "I still try to read all the negative reviews. What customers hate and wish for drive our further innovations."

Of course, gathering feedback is one thing; deciding what to do with it is another. Similar to our work to understand the original problem, we have to consider the customer feedback in terms of cost v. benefit. Are customers suggesting a minor tweak, easily incorporated into production, that enhances the Value Prop? Are they asking for attributes that might be better included in a future release? Or, are we simply dealing with one person's opinion, as opposed to a market consensus? We want to add value, but we also need to avoid knee-jerk reactions that upset the momentum we are building!

Make Pricing Adjustments

Pricing is dynamic, but should always tie back to the Value Prop. How much better is our product or solution at addressing the customer's Root Want compared to the Next Best Alternative? During the Growth phase, we expect to learn much more about all these factors. In actuality, how well does our product really solve the customer's problem? What is the Next Best Alternative? Has it changed since we identified our product for development? Since we launched it? Is the alternative a better option than we realized? Is it worse? What are we finding through direct observation of our product in-use?

We want to know the exact, quantifiable answers to these questions, but in reality, we may only have qualitative ideas. Customer adoption may be faster or slower than we expected, and the underlying reason may be complicated or even seem irrational. We may only see a symptom, not the underlying cause, so we need to continually assess whether we have the right price based on the market response.

Enhance Operational Excellence

During Launch, we executed an iterative process to balance supply with demand. During Growth, this balance continues to be critically important, along with other operational factors.

Service the Emerging Demand

As we grow the demand for our product, we must ensure that capacity and product availability keep pace. Mismanaging our supply, quality or cost position can severely handicap the product commercially and erode or kill the Business Case.

During Growth, our Value Prop is resonating with target customers. We initially enjoy a period of high price premium because we have the best solution to a customer problem. We have exclusivity. We want to maximize our sales during the period of expanding demand. How frustrating would it be for the customer if they bought into the Value Prop, saw our product as a real solution to a real problem, gained consensus internally, only to find out the product is not available? We do not want to give eager customers a reason *not* to buy our product! As with Launch, we don't want any self-inflicted wounds.

In order to ensure availability, it is critical to continually update the capacity v. demand forecast we created during Launch. Are customers converting as expected? Is capacity coming online as expected? Is everything going as planned? Do we have the ability to cover any anticipated capacity shortfalls, such as building inventory or "pulling forward" the capacity plan? As previously mentioned, all capacity decisions should be justified based on Return on Investment. However...don't run out of capacity in a Growth phase!

Improve Quality and Drive Down Costs

During Launch, we tolerated higher production costs because gaining commercial traction is the primary objective. This continues to be true in the Growth phase because we do not want to miss this wave of sales while we have a competitive advantage. First Revenue, then cost. However, profitability now begins to be a larger consideration. Despite growing sales, we almost certainly will need to improve costs in order to achieve the Business Case that we used to justify the product in the first place. We also cannot carry a bad cost position into Maturity, where lower prices lead to minimal margins, even with a good cost position. While we are growing our commercial position, we must also begin a serious focus on improving product costs. We expect cost improvement as we start to realize economies of scale and as projects are identified and completed to improve manufacturing efficiencies. Specific areas of cost focus are discussed in more detail in the next chapter.

In addition, we expect to gain a better understanding of the product that allows us to build-in quality and reduce scrap. During the Launch phase we probably incorporated higher product inspection rates to prevent defective products from reaching the customer. However, these inspections are bad for cost for two reasons. First, the inspections themselves have an inherent cost. We have to pay the inspector, and we have to add the inspections as process steps in manufacturing, increasing production cycle time. Second, inspections do not *prevent* poor quality products from being produced; they only prevent the defective products from reaching the customers. A defective product found during inspection must be reworked or scrapped. So, although an inspection-based quality system may protect the customer, it still leads to higher internal costs. Also, it is worth noting that inspection systems will not be 100% effective, especially if they rely on statistical sampling plans. A better approach is to understand the key process parameters that ensure the product attributes are within specification, and then control these process parameters to prevent defective product from ever being produced. This eliminates the inspection cost, the scrap cost, and still protects the customer and our commercial position. This starts to become important during Growth, and is absolutely essential during Maturity. One focus of the Product Team is to ensure Manufacturing is working toward improved costs, without putting our commercial position at risk!

Compendium
- Maximize the Growth phase. It is the best time of a product's life.
- Selling more to existing customers is the most effective and efficient way to grow.
- Promote! Evangelize the Value Prop to expand demand.
- Expand the channel strategy and look for adjacencies.
- Aggressively defend against the competitive response with IP, branding and a clear commercial message.
- Develop the ecosystem to entrench the product.
- Fine tune the price based on market adoption and a continual reassessment of the Value Prop.
- Look for opportunities to improve the product. What are the users saying?
- Ensure product availability. Don't miss the demand wave.
- Improve quality and drive down costs to maximize profitability and prepare for Maturity.

Chapter 8
MATURITY

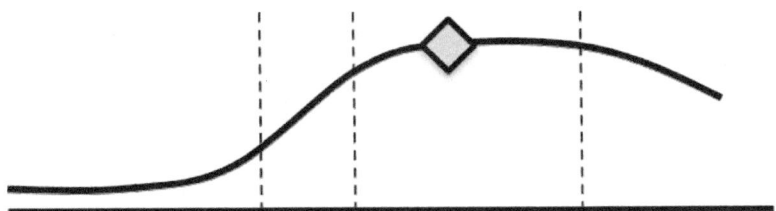

"Yesterday's home runs don't win today's games." Babe Ruth

Growth is the golden age in a product lifecycle. We enjoy the expanding demand and a high price premium during an initial era of exclusivity. Unfortunately, the more successful we are, the more the competitors will want a piece of the market. Nothing is exclusive for long. Profitability invites competition. Although we don't like it, the competitors are here. Despite our best efforts to proclaim the Value Prop and enforce barriers to entry, we now find sales flattening as we enter the Mature phase.

But, it wasn't just the competitors who brought us here. The customers also played a part. Customers, after all, have their own operations to consider. They increasingly want to leverage multiple suppliers in order to drive down prices and achieve assurance of supply. As they increase volume, they certainly want better pricing. The customers *want to see the product commoditized.*

During Growth we focused primarily on maximizing top line sales. Now, with Revenue flattening, we turn our attention to total costs to maximize Gross Margin dollars while we determine how to position the product in the new market reality.

Situational Assessment

As we said earlier, making good decisions depends on our starting point. It's obvious when we are in the Launch phase, because we are…well, *Launching*. Growth is apparent as well based on the rapid, disproportionate rate at which sales are expanding. Maturity can be a little trickier. Not only can the onset of the phase be more difficult to recognize, we might also be in denial. The organization does not want to believe the product is no longer in Growth. The organization wants trees that grow to the sky.

"You are here" - Indications of Product Maturity

In order to act appropriately for a product in the Mature phase, we first have to recognize and acknowledge that is where we are. As noted earlier, this is one reason we track Revenue instead of unit volume as the primary product lifecycle indicator. Unit volume may continue to increase in the Mature phase, but that does not necessarily mean we are still in Growth. Price pressure can offset (or worse!) the volume growth, causing our Revenue to flatten or even fall as the unit volume continues to grow. Consider the example of the iPad.

Figure 8.1   iPad Revenue and Volume, 2010 - 2018

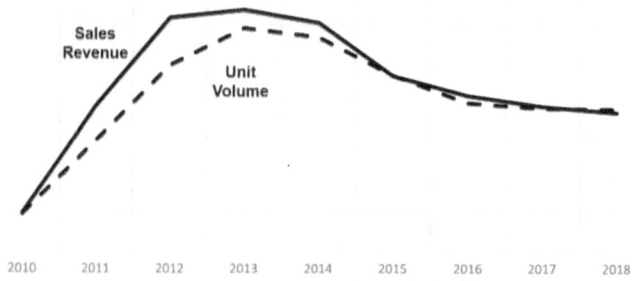

Figure 8.1 is a graph of iPad Sales Revenue and Unit Volume by year, from 2010 to 2018. As indicated by the dotted line, the Unit Volume continues to indicate growth through 2013. In fact, Apple sold 22% more iPads in 2013 compared to 2012. It would be very tempting to treat this as a continuation of the Growth phase. However, the Sales Revenue curve (solid line) clearly indicates that 2012 was the last year of Growth, as the emergence of competition in the tablet market drove

the iPad into Maturity by 2013. Volume growth was offset by price declines, resulting in flat Revenue. The Product Manager must understand and acknowledge the current reality in order to take the appropriate business actions. Volume growth can be misleading!

It is worth noting that, in general, product lifecycles are getting shorter as a result of technology and widespread, global competition. The iPad was an innovative product. However, if we consider Apple launched the iPad in 2010, and 2013 is the first year of Maturity, we see Apple enjoyed only two years of Growth! The speed of competition makes it even more important to recognize the indications that our product may have moved into Maturity. Also, the iPad sales follow a fairly characteristic lifecycle curve, but our product may not be as textbook. Recall the sales history of compact discs from earlier. It can be difficult to recognize the transition from Growth to Maturity, so we should be aware of the typical indications of a Mature product:

- Many competitors have entered the market, possibly including offshore suppliers and generics competing primarily on price.
- Prices begin to stabilize at a low-profit equilibrium point as the market saturates with suppliers.
- Terms and conditions of supply contracts increasingly favor the customer, including longer warranty periods, delivery commitments, and built-in price reductions.
- Customers place more emphasis on lead time, price, assurance of supply, and standardization, and less emphasis on innovation and differentiation. Differentiation may even be discouraged.
- Switching costs and barriers to entry for new suppliers are low, as industry standards are increasingly used to specify product requirements, capabilities, and constructions.
- There may be new solutions or technologies emerging that threaten to displace our product (e.g., CDs replaced vinyl).

Viability: How do we fit in the Corporate Strategy?

Although not as dynamic as the Growth phase, there is still money to be made in Maturity. Many product lines have long, profitable Mature cycles, generating Revenue and grinding out profit for the companies that stick with them and the Product Managers who run them well. You may just want to keep this product around for a while. But make no mistake; managing a product in Maturity is a challenge. Before we can go too far with putting forth our plan for the product, we first have to understand how our Mature product fits into the company strategy. This is important throughout the lifecycle, but most important in the Mature phase, as we start to make decisions about where to go from here. A Product Manager should always have a ready answer to the questions, "Why does the company have your product line? Why do we have *you*?" In the Growth phase, the answer is easy, and typically comes from the financial growth projections for the product. That is, we generate a lot of Revenue and profit, and expect to do more in the future. In the Mature phase, that answer may no longer hold water. Some possible reasons to maintain a Mature product might include:

- Though not growing, the product continues to generate significant amounts of Revenue for the company and enables us to maintain our manufacturing footprint, personnel, and capabilities.
- The product generates profit (positive GM) to pay for corporate overhead and to fund product development, possibly for other product lines.
- The product is a necessary part of an overall portfolio, and "pulls through" other, more profitable and/or growing products. Cable TV providers, for example, may need to offer local channels and the major networks in order to also sell premium channels.
- There is reason to believe the product can again achieve differentiation and preference in the market.
- There is reason to believe the product can grow Sales Revenue through adjacencies.
- The market is expected to grow again. For example, if government funding is expected to be available in the future. (Remember to look at the Market Environment!)

We must be very honest about the purpose and outlook for the product. It is easy to develop a sentimental attachment to a product that has been successful in the past, but our decisions must always be forward-looking. Many products are labeled as "strategic," but ultimately, strategy must translate to the P&L. We have to see a clear connection between our product and financial returns for the company.

Managing the Product: Maximize Gross Margin Dollars

Throughout Launch and Growth, we focused primarily on topline Revenue. While it is true costs always matter, the favorable commercial environment during these phases led to a push for maximum sales. Revenue before cost, as we said earlier. Now, as competitors have arrived, exclusivity has ended, prices have fallen, and the resulting margins no longer justify this absolute focus on sales. We now need a more holistic view of the product line P&L, so we shift our focus to Gross Margin dollars as the bellwether metric for our Mature product.

Commercial
Differentiation v. Cost of Complexity

To do well commercially with a Mature product, we prefer to compete on something *other than* price. We want to look for sources of differentiation compared to the competition. Even in Maturity, a commodity market is not necessarily the end of product differentiation. Although this may seem to be a contradiction of terms, many products are able to introduce features and attributes which continue to achieve differentiation through improved user experience. Differentiation can still be translated into a product preference or, in some cases, even a price premium.

For example, is there anything more commoditized than a standard handheld potato peeler? Yet, OXO offers their Good Grips® Pro Swivel potato peeler with a large, ergonomic grip, and it recently listed for 3x the price of a standard potato peeler at a major US retailer. It is used in the same application, by the same market, yet achieves a price premium because of the improved user experience. Or, consider another highly commoditized product, the standard #2 wooden pencil. Mechanical pencils, which serve the same function, recently listed for 2x the price of the wooden version at a major US office supply store. "Low resistance" golf tees and "strike anywhere" matches are other examples of differentiation in commodity markets. There are "enhanced" cardboard boxes. You can even pay well over $100 for a highly advanced, metal alloy yoyo!

Enhanced user experience is one method of achieving differentiation in the Mature phase, but it is not the only way. What do the customers value other than price? Is a short lead time important, or our ability to respond to an unforecast demand spike? Do they value environmentally-friendly "green" packaging, or perhaps 24x7 field support? Are there customizations we can easily add to the product which will be valued by the customer? Do they want a racing stripe, a matte finish, or their name, phone number and web address in raised white letters?

If we can find a source of differentiation, even if it is modest or cosmetic, what is it worth? Do we want to shoot for a price premium, as in the example of the potato peeler, or do we want to command a preference v. the competitors? Presumably, if the retailer priced the OXO Good Grips potato peeler at the same price as the standard product, there would be an overwhelming preference for the more ergonomic version. The Product Manager must consider several factors, such as the price elasticity of demand, the short and long-term market outlook, the competitive products and capabilities, the impact on cost, and other relevant factors when determining how to best leverage the differentiation. In general, of course, we prefer a price premium. However, because it can be hard to justify to the customer the value of differentiation in a commoditized market, it is often more realistic to obtain a product preference, which can help us continue to survive as the market thins out the suppliers.

Differentiation, however, is a two-sided coin, and the commercial benefit of differentiation may be offset by the impact on operational costs. This is especially true if the differentiation is achieved by customizing the product. Customization is, simply, bad for costs. The "cost of complexity" can exceed the commercial benefit, so it must be understood in order to make informed product decisions. Customized products can affect production costs if they require special materials, take longer to setup in manufacturing, have smaller lot sizes, include additional process steps, or require special operator skills. They typically have an adverse effect on inventory costs at all levels, from raw materials, to work-in-process, to non-conforming product, to finished goods. What's more, it can be very difficult to capture an accurate cost of customization. While the *benefit* of a price premium is readily reflected in the margin, the *true cost* of complexity may not be.

As we are looking for sources of differentiation, we are also combing the product line to find existing variants that are adversely affecting our cost position. Most likely, our sales-centric view of the world in Growth has led to a proliferation of product variants that are no longer profitable. In the Mature phase, we prune away the variations that adversely impact the product line P&L at the Gross Margin line.

If the commercial benefit of the SKU (product variant) does not justify the cost of complexity (and impact on capacity), it is a prime candidate to be removed from the product offering. A review of the historical Sales Revenue, volume, and profitability of our SKUs will typically reveal which are the contributors, and which are dragging us down.

It may seem to be a contradiction that we talk about adding complexity for differentiation while we also talk about pruning the tail of the distribution. Just to be clear, it is not easy to achieve differentiation in Maturity. Many customers won't value it. Or, at a minimum, they won't acknowledge the value. In addition, it is not easy to rationalize the benefit of differentiation v. the impact on cost. In Maturity, we only want to manufacture the best, most profitable versions of the product line, as measured by Gross Margin. It is the responsibility of the Product Team, and especially the Product Manager, to understand the cost v. benefit tradeoff and make informed decisions about the product portfolio.

Price Sensitivity, Even with Lower Price Pressure

With or without product differentiation, pricing continues to be critical in the Mature phase. Products typically experience extensive price erosion during Growth. The iPad of the previous example experienced >10% year-over-year price pressure every year until the market stabilized in Maturity. This price pressure invariably leads to low profitability. That is, as long as margins are attractive, competitors will continue to enter the market, and price will continue to erode. Although the magnitude of price pressure in Maturity is probably no longer double-digit percentages, as it often is in Growth, even minor price erosion can be too much for the already-thin margins. The market will not see price stabilization until the business becomes unattractive to new entrants. Price stability comes when suppliers are no longer willing or able to make large price concessions in exchange for market share.

However, relative price stability should not be confused with price insensitivity. Recall that switching costs are low in a mature market as a result of standardization. If the products are viewed as commodities by the customers, then even small price differences will influence the customer's sourcing decisions. This is also why it is typically more reasonable for a Mature product to achieve a preference with product differentiation, as opposed to a price premium. Setting a higher price point that isn't very clearly justified by our level of differentiation and *acknowledged* by the customer will lead to lower Sales Revenue and lower market share. However, offering a better product at the same price, even if the benefit is qualitative, can achieve a preference.

In a Mature market, we have to be competitive on price, but we do not want to be the price leader. Find a way to compete on something other than price.

Sellout the Capacity to Improve Manufacturing Costs

As mentioned, our primary financial goal during Maturity is to maximize Gross Margin dollars, and this means we need high volume to improve our cost position. Specifically, maximizing Gross Margin dollars means selling all the capacity from the manufacturing footprint. As we already noted, setting a price point too high in a commoditized market leads to lower Revenue and lower volume. Lower volume leads to higher per-unit Variable Costs due to inefficient use of labor and materials, and due to lack of scale. Furthermore, with Sales volume less than capacity, the Fixed Assets are not fully loaded, and the Fixed Costs are not fully absorbed. In the end, we have lower Gross Margin dollars, which is the primary metric for a Mature product. To put this more simply, if Fixed Costs are truly "fixed," at least in the short term, then maximizing *Gross Margin* dollars means maximizing *Variable Margin* dollars, which in turn means maximizing profitable Sales.

Of course, selling out our capacity is easier said than done, especially when the competition has the same goal. Also, this is very much a market-dependent issue, and really starts to cross over into Market strategy from Product Management. However, some general guidance to consider:

- Securing long term contracts and supply agreements with large customers can lead to a more accurate forecasting process and more stable demand profile. It also enables better customer intimacy. If market demand is concentrated at a few customers, then strong contract positions are critical.
- In highly fragmented markets, increased use of Distributors can have the effect of consolidating demand, making numerous small customers appear like a single, large customer. A Distributor that adds value for the customer, such as stocking of product, product bundling, or value-added services, can also help create a source of differentiation.

- In some cases, spot markets exist, and can be an outlet for otherwise idle capacity. However, be prepared for pricing in the spot market to be extremely competitive.

Operations
Drive to Lowest Cost Position

Sales is one part of the equation for maximizing Gross Margin dollars; cost is the other. During Launch and Growth, we tolerated the higher costs associated with a new, low volume product because capturing the Revenue was the most important consideration. We were in a phase in the lifecycle where product availability mattered more than cost. In Maturity, the focus has shifted. Now we expect to be in an environment with many competitors, with decreased pricing driving lower margins, where customers are increasingly unwilling to pay for differentiation. The P&L focus necessarily shifts from top line Revenue to Gross Margin. We must get to a cost position that allows reasonable profitability for the continued viability of the product. While the Product Manager does not directly control cost reduction, we must exert leadership and influence through the Product Team to ensure projects and priorities are oriented toward achieving the lowest competitive cost. This means going through the P&L statement from top to bottom, and looking for opportunities to improve every single line. Where to look:

Variable Cost, Materials

- Material substitution projects to replace higher cost materials with lower cost alternatives. Can metallic parts be replaced with plastic without impacting performance?
- Use of commodity grade materials in place of custom or specialty materials. Are recycled materials an option with our customers?
- Projects to improve material utilization by consistently running product dimensions at the design nominal.
- Technology or Engineering projects to reduce the nominal material dimensions.
- Implementation of a comprehensive, build-in approach to quality that replaces inspections. This is accomplished by first understanding the key product attributes and dimensions that ensure product performance. Next, process settings and

tolerances are mapped to the key product attributes. Process settings are then controlled in such a manner that consistent product is produced. This eliminates inspection cost and reduces scrap associated with non-conforming products.

- Specific projects focused on reducing scrap.

Variable Cost, Labor

- Increase production line speeds and reduce setup times.
- Improve first pass yield. Scrapped product contains labor cost, not just material cost, and remakes are an inefficient use of available capacity.
- Optimize lot sizes to achieve lower per-unit costs through improvement of the planning and scheduling processes.
- Implement process automation, especially for non-value-added processes, such as material movement via Autonomous Guided Vehicles (AGVs).
- Review Make v. Buy decisions on components and sub-assemblies. Can we save money by outsourcing certain components? Alternatively, can we save money and improve asset utilization by making some components we currently buy, and vertically integrating the supply chain?
- Utilize a lower skilled, lower cost labor force via process simplification, error-proofing, and build-in quality.

Unfortunately, many cost reductions require projects or investments that may not be justified considering the profitability and long-term viability of the product. Process automation to reduce labor costs in manufacturing may require investments of capital and resources that are prohibitive based on the payback period and the willingness of Management to commit to a Mature product line. Undertaking projects such as these also ties directly back to our place in the corporate strategy.

Fixed Cost, Depreciation

It is entirely possible that our product volume is increasing while our Sales Revenue remains roughly flat. This makes many Fixed Cost decisions difficult. The long-term forecast may indicate we need more lines to support the volume, which can also generate more Revenue. However, more lines mean more Depreciation. More lines may also mean more Engineers to support them, more utility cost to run them, and a bigger building to house them. Our goal in the Mature phase should be to maximize the output of the manufacturing footprint. To do more with less. It is not about what we want, nor even about what we think we need. It is about what we can *afford*.

Improvements to line speed, setup time, lot size, and first pass yield not only improve Variable Costs, they also improve Fixed Costs by reducing the amount of equipment we need to meet the demand forecast. By accomplishing these improvements, we can potentially avoid burdening the P&L with Fixed Costs that we may not be able to afford. In addition, we may be able to write-off unused or seldom-used equipment, and even shrink our manufacturing footprint.

Fixed Cost, Headcount

IT support, Engineers, Supervision, and others are all part of the manufacturing costs. We would not suggest leaving the product to atrophy, but we must seek to minimize the Fixed Cost headcount that supports its production. Product standardization and elimination of unprofitable, undifferentiated product variations can reduce the Fixed staffing needed to support the volume, and should be considered when assessing the profitability of the SKUs that comprise the product portfolio.

Corporate Overhead (Below the GM line)

Our product is also responsible for funding a portion of the corporate overhead, such as Sales, Marketing, Technology, and Product Management. Again, we must consider what we can afford, v. what we might like to have. And, although this falls below the GM line on the P&L, many Product Managers are still responsible for the profitability at this level.

Technology: Mature products should require very little ongoing support from the Technology organization. If we are continuing to introduce new product features and attributes, we again must ensure that the commercial benefits they deliver, such as price premium or customer preference, clearly justify the incremental Technology spend.

Marketing: Similarly, we would not expect to continue to promote Mature products. All the essential Marketing collateral should be in place long before the product reaches Maturity. Customers should know about the product. Although some promotional costs may be associated with the introduction of a new attribute, and some ongoing maintenance costs might be expected, there should be minimal Marketing spend.

(At this point, we should see that product attributes for differentiation carry many elements of cost with them, so the commercial benefit should be carefully scrutinized.)

Selling: How are customers buying the product? Sales should not require extensive effort for a Mature product in a commoditized market. The applications and uses of the product should be well understood, and we would expect that we are now taking orders rather than engaging in active selling. Depending on the customer base, we might consider alternatives to the cost of maintaining an active sales force, such as:

- If not already in place, e-commerce can reduce product overhead costs. For Mature products that are well-understood by the customers, online ordering without personal interaction can be faster, easier, and less costly. An investment in a positive e-commerce experience could be a huge benefit and cost savings.
- Commission-based rep firms: Can we service the customer demand using commission-based selling in place of a full-time sales force?
- Increased use of distribution channels to consolidate demand and reduce overhead costs.

Are we sure? The Importance of an Accurate P&L

Of course, all of this assumes we have an accurate P&L. We must understand our product line profitability to make good decisions. More than in any other lifecycle phase, the accuracy of the P&L is critically important in the Mature phase. While it is relatively easy (and fun) to count the new product Revenue during Launch and Growth, now we are focused primarily on making long-term, short-term, and even day-to-day decisions based on margins. In some cases, where product margins are exceptionally thin, inaccurate costing could be the difference between making and losing money. If we don't accurately know our costs, we really don't know anything. Just as we took a top-to-bottom look at the P&L for opportunities to improve costs, so too we should take a similar look to verify accuracy.

The first consideration is the accuracy of Variable Costs. Variable Labor, material consumption rates, and, to a certain extent, scrap, are typically captured in Bills of Material (BOM) and Work Center Routings used by a Manufacturing Execution System (MES) to facilitate manufacturing of and accounting for products. Over a long period of time manufacturing a particular product, these values should become more accurate, as the manufacturing team has opportunities to measure, analyze, and improve the performance. However, the improvements may not always be reflected in the production standards. Old assumptions about line speeds or setup times may remain in place unless a dedicated effort is made to evaluate actual performance v. theoretical on a regular basis. Without periodic validation and update, production standards can become out-of-sync with actual performance, and the standard cost of the product will become inaccurate.

Similarly, depending on the standards and preferences in place, the BOMs and Routings may reflect some standard allowance for scrap. Various assumptions about startup losses or product yield may be incorporated into the standard cost. First, it is worth knowing what accounting standards are used, and if any allowance for scrap is included in the standard cost. Also, inaccuracies in production standards don't simply disappear. They are captured as production variances. If the product runs "better" than the standard, this will typically be accounted for by the plant as a variance, and the standard cost in the system will be higher than the actual cost of manufacturing. Alternatively, and much more commonly, the product may run worse than the standard due to inefficiencies, wait times, and poor quality. In these cases, the standard cost reflected in the system will be lower than the actual, true cost. Either way, without considering the production variances, and the reasons for them, we cannot understand our true product cost, and we cannot make good product decisions, especially regarding pricing.

In addition, assumptions about line speed, line setup time, average production lot size, and other manufacturing parameters often drive not just costing, but also capacity calculations. If our standard cost is wrong, our assumed capacity is probably wrong as well. For the Product Manager of a Mature product, it is well worth investing the time with the Finance team to understand what assumptions are included in the standards, when and how they are updated, and what variances we are seeing.

Another consideration in our quest for an accurate P&L is the extent to which the product line is burdened with cost in a shared factory. That is, if more than one product is manufactured in our factory, is the split of material and labor correct in the respective product P&Ls? Especially, we should consider the accuracy of the Fixed Cost allocations. If equipment is shared among multiple products, the allocation of depreciation may not accurately reflect utilization. The same is true for the allocation of Fixed Labor costs, such as Engineers, Manufacturing Supervisors, and Plant Staff. Further, cost associated with the building itself should be accurately allocated, such as utilities, building depreciation, insurance, taxes, and environmental permitting. It is possible, and in fact, likely, that standards were determined at an earlier point in time, and do not reflect the current situation. It is an important reality check to consider that many Plant Managers and Plant Controllers are most concerned with total plant costs, which they are directly responsible for, and are less concerned with the allocation of these costs among the various products, which they may see as an arbitrary "left pocket / right pocket" exercise. While achieving correct cost allocations does not, in and of itself, reduce total costs for the company, it does impact our product line profitability, and therefore our product line decisions. If our product line is overly burdened with Fixed Costs, we will see a distorted view of profitability on the P&L. This may lead us to make bad product decisions, and even obsolesce a product, in an extreme case. Only then might we realize that the Fixed Costs we carried cannot be eliminated with the product.

In a similar manner, Technology and Corporate overhead allocations may follow outdated or even arbitrary assumptions. Inaccuracies almost certainly exist in this area. Ideally, the product P&L would only reflect those costs inherent to designing, developing, making and selling it. However, instead of this "bottoms up" approach, it is common to use a "top down" approach, which takes the total Technology and Corporate costs, and allocates them to products based on some figure of merit which may or may not reflect reality. For example, Sales and Marketing costs may be allocated to products based on the percentage of total corporate Revenue each represents. This may not reflect the true, inherent cost of selling our product. When our product is Mature, and well understood by the market, customers may be ordering from a contract, purchase agreement, or via a web portal, with little or no real Sales interaction or cost. Bad cost assumptions feeding the P&L may again lead to bad decisions for the product.

Extending Maturity

Once we have rationalized the product portfolio by considering commercial benefit v. operational costs, and minimized costs from top to bottom in the P&L, and ensured P&L accuracy, we may be at a profitability position we can live with. We may want to extend this period as long as we can, generating Revenue and margin while we search for the Next Big Thing. Assuming we have also captured everything we can through contracts, use of Distributors, and even sales in the spot market, we would look for other ways to increase demand. Some options to consider would include regional adjacencies, market adjacencies, and product rebranding. While these avenues may raise Revenue year-over-year, we should realize that we are not necessarily in another Growth cycle, per se. We are still in a commoditized market; the addressable size of the market has simply grown.

Now, a return to a new Growth cycle would be optimal at this point! In the consumer space, we sometimes see fashion products and fads with multiple Growth cycles, but these are typically driven by market demand cycles rather than any product activities. In the B2B space, we almost certainly need a new and significant source of differentiation that opens additional opportunities for the product by addressing a new unmet customer need.

However, if volume demand remains strong, and if we can secure the lowest cost position in the market, possibly with some source of differentiation for price or preference, then we may be able to have a long, profitable Maturity phase. While competitive forces have pushed price and margins down, there may still be significant Revenue and Gross Margin dollars to grab. Low loss optical fiber was invented over 45 years ago, but copper communications cables are still sold. And someone is still out there making and selling wooden #2 pencils and standard potato peelers.

Compendium

- Competitors will continue to enter the market and drive down price as long as it is profitable to do so. Market prices eventually stabilize when margins are too low to be attractive to new entrants.
- Mature products often fit within a company's strategy as long as they continue to generate Revenue and Gross Margin dollars.
- Differentiation can sometimes be achieved in a commoditized market through product features and attributes that improve user experience.
- Differentiation can also be achieved by offering support services, advantaged packaging, superior service, or other elements valued by the customer.
- In a commoditized market, differentiation can occasionally be leveraged to achieve a price premium, but is more typically used to gain market share through customer preference.
- Gross Margin dollars (GM$) is the bellwether metric for Mature products, and should be maximized by selling-out the manufacturing capacity at the highest price that can be justified based on differentiation, and by achieving the minimal cost position based on line-by-line review of the P&L.
- Productivity improvements reduce variable labor costs while improving fixed asset utilization.
- Projects to reduce cost should focus on material substitution, productivity improvements, and scrap elimination.
- A "build-in" approach to quality reduces scrap costs while eliminating inspection costs, and is essential for a Mature product.
- Investigate manufacturing standards, production variances, and cost allocations in the product P&L to ensure true understanding of the product profitability.

Chapter 9
DECLINE AND OBSOLESCENCE

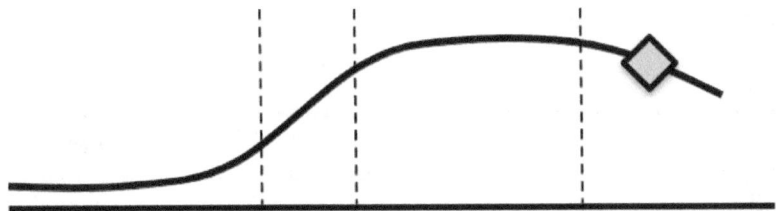

"He's dead, Jim." Dr. McCoy, Star Trek

Let's review how we got here.

Our product began as an unmet need in the mind of a customer. By solving the customer's problem, with a solution that addressed the Root Want better than the Next Best Alternative, we were able to Launch our product at a premium. As the product gained traction, we saw market "pull," and our investments in evangelizing the Value Prop produced disproportionate returns. Life was good, and our primary focus was on maximizing sales during this period of exclusivity. Of course, our success invited a competitive response. Despite our best efforts to establish strong barriers to entry, the Bad Guys brought FUD, and competing solutions, and lower prices. We experienced extensive price erosion, as competitive offerings continued to enter the market as long as the margins were attractive. Furthermore, the customers pushed for standardization and qualified the other suppliers in order to gain price leverage and assurance of supply. This drove the product into Maturity, where we shifted the primary focus from Sales to Gross Margin dollars as the most critical P&L metric. We poured our energy into two key efforts to keep the product viable:

1. Identify sources of differentiation that added more commercial benefit than operational costs, allowing us to compete on

something other than price
2. Focus on improving EVERY COST on the P&L

If we were successful in these endeavors, the product can continue to have a long and profitable life in Maturity. If not, we see Revenue and Margin continuing to fall year-over-year. The Value Prop is no longer sustained. The product is in Decline, and unless we can find a way to return it to an earlier lifecycle stage, we will need to determine our exit strategy. In order to do that, we must know a bit more about the market forces that put us here. What exactly is killing our product? What really changed?

Decline

There are many reasons a product can be in Decline and potentially sliding toward Obsolescence, but they really boil down to just a few underlying situations. For each of these, we should consider whether it is a temporary condition, or a permanent "new normal" that will continue to impact the product for the foreseeable future. Understanding the root cause and its permanence will help clarify where we go from here.

1. The market is still there, but we now have a better product we prefer to sell
    This is the best scenario. In essence, we have invented digital music and our CD sales are now suffering. In this case, we want to transition customers to our new Launch/Growth product and manage the demise of the current product.

2. The market is still there, but we are not competitive, and are losing share and volume
    It could be that a competitor has introduced a better product. Or, it could be that we can't compete on price, or quality, or supply, or features, or other attributes the customers value. Decreasing volume can quickly turn into a death spiral: lower volume ➔ under-utilized assets ➔ worse efficiencies ➔ higher costs ➔ less ability to respond to price pressure ➔ lower volume...
    There are any number of specific factors that can cause us to be uncompetitive, including:
    - The price pressure is just too high. This often comes from

offshore suppliers or generic substitutes, driving the market price to the point the business is no longer of interest to us.

- Increased material costs from our suppliers. This might happen due to changes in commodity prices, such as oil prices impacting the cost of plastic resins, or due to scarcity. Scarcity might occur if our material suppliers see better opportunities from other, more profitable market sectors. For example, DuPont's Kevlar is used in numerous products and markets, including ballistics applications (body armor), automotive components (hoses, belts, brake pads, tires), as well as for use in ropes and cables, and many other products and applications. A surge in demand from the most profitable market segment could lead to a shortage and/or price increase for the other segments. While these scenarios may not be permanent, the duration can be challenging to estimate, and the problem can certainly recur.

- Despite standardization efforts, cost reductions and pruning the product line, too much cost remains. Perhaps our product is highly customized, or volume has shrunk so much that even the standard products look like "specials." This can impact manufacturing costs and asset utilization. Or, maybe we just aren't very good at making it, and don't see a path to improvement.

Without a clear path to profitably gain volume and share, we are headed toward Obsolescence.

3. The market is still there, but our product no longer fits with the corporate strategy

Most large companies produce more than one product, and each product must be justified internally against financial expectations of the company. If we can't increase price enough or lower costs enough to achieve the profit expectations, we might be living on borrowed time. While it is not the corporate expectations that put us into Decline, those expectations may be the reason we take the next step to Obsolescence. Not every company wants to sell #2 wooden pencils. In addition to the items noted above affecting our ability to be competitive, we also may find internal hurdles:

- The product assets may be better utilized elsewhere. Sometimes there is a better corporate use for our building, machines, and people. For the good of the company, our product might need to step aside.

- Continued production may require investment. Assets don't last forever. We may find ourselves in a situation where continuing to produce the product means we have to recapitalize the factory, and we just can't financially justify it.

4. The market is leaving, or has already left

We might be doing everything right. We might be holding or gaining market share. We might have minimized costs. However, if the market is declining, or even disappearing, we may find ourselves in the wrong place at the wrong time. Recall the Market Environment discussion from the chapter on Product Planning. Market factors never cease to be important. It could be that these factors have now turned against us with challenging, or even insurmountable headwinds. Perhaps the source of funding is gone. For example, the demand for the product may have been rooted in a government stimulus program, which has now ended. Or, perhaps legal and regulatory changes have essentially legislated our product out of the market. New federal emissions standards might, for example, have made our version of the catalytic converter irrelevant. It might also be that macroeconomic factors have turned against us. If our product is sold as a component in luxury yachts, a recession could put a considerable damper on demand. It might also be that the underlying need is just gone. Many civil defense products were sold during the Cold War, such as gas masks. The end of the Cold War effectively eliminated the demand for these types of items.

Of course, as we have already alluded many times, we may just be the latest in the long list of casualties to new and improved technology. The transistor killed the vacuum tube; the DVD killed the video tape; the computer killed the typewriter; video killed the radio star, and there is no going back.

Actions

As you may have already noted, the forces that put the product in Decline are not easily reversed. In most cases, Decline is the path and Obsolescence is the unavoidable destination. While we are in Decline, however, we must do what we can to manage the profitability of the product:

- Consider raising price. Either customers will pay the price, potentially solving our profitability problem, or they will look for alternatives, potentially saving us the difficult task of discontinuing the product against their objections.
- Evaluate opportunities to outsource manufacturing in order to lower costs and eliminate fixed assets, while potentially salvaging the commercial position and Revenue stream.
- Further prune the product line to eliminate the least profitable SKUs. We began this effort in the Mature phase, but Decline forces it to another level. Consider offering only completely standardized products with no customization.
- If there is a niche market for highly specialized products, such as $100 yoyos, then manage these variations separately from the product that is in Decline.
- Manage inventory and the supply chain carefully to reduce inventory carrying costs and the risk of stranded / obsolete inventory in the form of raw materials, sub-assemblies, or finished products.
- Minimize product investment via rigorous application of ROI rules. We should not be investing in a product in Decline, and application of ROI rules will justify this position.
- Establish exit criteria and periodically evaluate our performance and the future outlook against these criteria. Just as we tracked performance against the Launch Plan, now we should be tracking performance relative to exit criteria.
- Minimize IP investment that does not clearly extend the life of the product. Consider selling the existing IP or licensing competitors as a form of cost recovery. (Note: be sure to consider all the potential impacts of this decision!)
- Promote selectively, and only when there is a clear path to profitably increasing sales.
- Consolidate distribution channels to achieve focus and again reduce the risk of stranded inventory.

Obsolescence

Sometimes demand for a product disappears. Often this is a result of new technology. Remember what happened to tapes and vinyl when the compact discs showed up. No amount of cost reduction or differentiation was going to save the audio cassette. The CD was simply a superior product. Sometimes there is no way to stop the Revenue slide. Sometimes it's just time to put an end to a product.

However, we cannot simply walk away from the product or the business. We have two high-level goals for Obsolescence:

- Salvage customers and customer relationships.
- Minimize the financial impact from discontinuing the product

Similar to Launch, Obsolescence requires a well-executed plan to avoid potentially dire consequences.

Salvage the Customers

The first and obvious issue, if we are truly obsolescing a product, is how to manage the customers. While the market and/or our share may have declined, the customers who account for the remaining Sales Revenue are still important. Although we have decided we no longer want to offer this product, we may need these customers again. We need a carefully considered approach, perhaps to protect sales of other products, and to protect the relationship for future products. What are we going to tell them? What do we want them to do?

First, they need to know what to buy in place of the old product. As mentioned previously, perhaps there is a 'new and improved' version that replaces the original product. In this case, the Obsolescence messaging and actions should be tied into the Launch of the new product. The messaging is important, but should not be difficult if the new product has a strong Value Prop.

Or, perhaps we want to substitute a standardized version of the product in place of the customized, low volume SKU they currently buy. We might propose the standard that "everyone else" buys. There is a risk in a commoditized market, with low switching costs, that the customer – OUR customer – will simply switch to another supplier. While that may not be the worst scenario for this product, we certainly want to minimize the collateral damage to other products we sell them, and to future opportunities.

Price is one way to manage the transition. For example, assume our company offers electrical drop cords in 50', 75', and 100' lengths, and we want to obsolesce the 75' version. Assuming we have already increased the price as described previously in Decline, now we can look at further reducing the price difference between the 75' and 100' versions. This may involve decreasing the price on the 100' version, and/or further increase on the 75' version. If we can make the prices comparable, the customer can now get (presumably) a better product at a similar price. We expect to get an improved cost position by eliminating a "special," as well as an increase in Revenue (and probably Margin).

Another option is to engage in a contract manufacturing or private labeling arrangement with another supplier. This allows us to continue to offer the product commercially and realize the Revenue at a small profit, without the complexity and cost of maintaining manufacturing operations. Selling or licensing IP to this supplier can help facilitate the relationship, making it a win-win for both parties. It may even be possible to sell our raw material, in-process, and finished goods inventory to them.

As a final scenario, it may be that we do not have a substitute product to propose. In the previous example, maybe we simply no longer want to offer electrical drop cords at all. In this case, we still want to minimize the damage to the customer relationship through measures such as:

- Offering a "last buy" opportunity. Consolidating these "last buys" from multiple customers into one final production run can have the added benefit of lowering costs through batch production, and can help reduce or eliminate unwanted inventory.
- Directing the customer to a Distributor who can provide a suitable substitute product.
- Consider directing the customer to a competitor who will continue to offer the product. This is risky! Even if we are exiting the product line, we should still be careful about facilitating the relationship between our customer and our competitor, which can be a huge long-term mistake.

Other subjects to address in the customer messaging should include:
- Availability of repair parts, if applicable.
- Backwards compatibility of any alternative or future products.
- Ongoing availability of product literature, safety instructions, and environmental impact information.
- At what price we *would* be willing to continue to sell the product. (We definitely will need a good answer for this question!)

Manage the Financial Impact

Obsolescence is not so different from Launch, in that we need a thorough, well-thought-out plan, followed by violent execution. Also similar to Launch, there are a lot of tactics and logistics to consider in the Obsolescence plan. The timing and interaction of these events needs to be carefully considered. These include:

- Stop quoting the old product. We don't want open quotes floating around the market as we are trying to discontinue a product.

- Notify customers. The customer management process mentioned above needs to be documented and thoroughly vetted. What is the timing? What are the product substitutes? We don't want the notification process to leave matters open-ended.

- What will we do with inventory at our Distributors? They will not want us to go to the market with a message of product Obsolescence while they are holding inventory for sale. Can they return unsold inventory? Will we offer an incentive to them to sell the remaining inventory? Are we going to give them an advantage on the new or substitute product?

- Handle internal "system" issues, such as "blocking" part numbers to prevent ordering.

- Review product collateral, such as spec sheets, catalogs, installation and operating procedures. Many of these items need to be available as long as the product is in the market, even if we have stopped selling it, but we also don't want customers ordering or specifying the old product based on this literature.

- We may have considerable cost tied up in raw materials, work-in-process, and finished goods inventories, as well as held or out-of-flow product. What do we intend to do with this? Will suppliers take back the raw materials? Can they be used in other products? How can we incentivize customers to buy the finished goods, without upsetting the market price for the replacement products, and without impacting the Distributors? What about the subassemblies? Do we scrap these, or do we create more finished goods, assuming we have an outlet? Were we able to outsource manufacturing to another supplier, and will they buy the inventory?

- Determine what to do with our IP portfolio. Do we still need it? If not, is there a cost recovery opportunity to sell patents or license a competitor? Can this facilitate a private labeling agreement?

- What are we going to do with the manufacturing assets? Will these be used for other products? We have approached this as a product obsolescence event, but we could consider completely exiting the business. We could consider selling the assets, the IP, the inventory, and everything associated with the business. That, however, is a discussion for another day.

Compendium

- A product can be in Decline due to a declining market, a bad cost position, an uncompetitive Value Prop, or any combination of these factors.
- Market forces that lead to Decline are difficult to reverse, and often lead to Obsolescence.
- The Product Obsolescence process should attempt to salvage customer relationships and minimize financial exposure.
- Similar to Launch, Obsolescence involves many moving parts, and requires a thorough plan and violent execution.
- Even after Obsolescence, some level of product support and documentation may be required.

TREES DON'T GROW TO THE SKY

AUTHOR'S NOTE
OF COURSE, IT'S NOT THAT SIMPLE

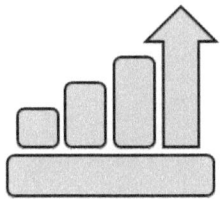

"Everything should be made as simple as possible, but not simpler."
Albert Einstein

I began this work with a discussion on the Product Management role, on the need to make good decisions, and the importance of understanding the fundamentals of the product lifecycle. The results we get depend on the decisions we make, and the decisions we make depend on where we are and where we want to go. Unfortunately, I could not produce a prescriptive narrative of how to behave in every possible instance. Products, markets, companies and people are all different. Situations are different. Goals and strategies are different. The only universal answer we can give is, "It depends."

What I have tried to do here is to capture *upon what* it depends. Though it is not possible to capture the totality of Product Management theory in a single text, I hope you find the discussions, examples, and insights useful in forming the basis you need to make informed Product Management decisions.

Because that's what success looks like.

www.ingramcontent.com/pod-product-compliance
Lightning Source LLC
Chambersburg PA
CBHW021448210526
45463CB00002B/682